# Why Not Me?

Lori J Miller

*Why Not Me?*


ISBN: 978-1-59352-341-1
Published by:
Christian Services Network
833 Broadway, Suite #201
El Cajon, CA 92021
Toll Free: 1-866-484-6184
www.CSNbooks.com



Some names have been changed in order to protect the idenity.

Printed in the United States of America.

# Dedication

This book is dedicated to Jodi L. Lind, fellow cancer patient and dear friend.

# Acknowledgment

Thank-you, Aunt Judy, for painstakingly and lovingly combing through the pages of this story to make it more understandable and interesting to the reader. Without your editing expertise, this would not be the quality of book that it is. Aunt Judy, your labor of love has not gone unnoticed. I can never repay you for your hard work, but I appreciate it more than you'll ever know. Thank you. I love you. -Lori

# Table of Contents

# Foreword

The title of this book begs another question, "Why would a beautiful, life-loving young wife and mother, three times diagnosed with cancer and enduring incredible suffering during the treatments, NOT ask 'WHY...?'" You will see the answer in page after page as Lori shares her experiences with incredible honesty and touches of humor: "God Himself lovingly orchestrates even the most difficult circumstances of the lives of His children, graciously accomplishing His purposes as He comforts with His presence." Her prayer is that God will use HER testimony to encourage and strengthen you on YOUR journey.

Carol (Gutwein) Kaptain

Lori Miller takes us on personal tour of her experiences with cancer, and shares how she, her family, friends and associates not only survived the same, but also gained from the experience. Lori not only provides insight into the physical, emotional, and psychological trauma of a cancer victim, she also directs our attention to the crucial spiritual dimension. I recommend this book to you for that very reason.

One could very easily become overly embroiled with the medical and physical debilitation of the story – it is most important to see/understand the role that a relationship with God played throughout. Lori, and her friend Jodi Lind, learned there was more to the journey than merely surviving cancer. It involved living the life only the Supreme Life Giver could provide. Perhaps you will find, through this story, that there is more to life than survival.

Pastor Terry Matlock,
Tabernacle of Praise, Eau Claire, WI

This author writes from her heart and her wealth of experience. As a fellow cancer patient of 32 years myself and a sister in the Lord, it is easy for me to understand Lori's heart and her burning desire to reach others where they are. Cancer is not easy but neither is life. We all have our challenges, hurts, battles, and struggles along the way but with Him as our partner and guide, you too can be a survivor like Lori and make a difference!

Rena Tarbet
Senior National Sales Director in Mary Kay

# Preface

"You have cancer." The words echoed off the walls of the doctor's office like the sound of a metal ball in a pinball machine spinning out of control. My world began to spin just as wildly. I know the doctor kept talking.

"Stage 2 ovarian cancer."

"We're lucky to have caught it in this early stage."

"We recommend six months of chemotherapy."

"I have referred you to a doctor. He would like to see you as soon as possible."

I am so glad Todd was there and actually paying attention. My world was whirling. I was unsuccessfully trying to wrap my mind around those three simple yet potentially life-shattering words, "You have cancer."

Dr. Sharpe got up from his chair and moved to shake Todd's hand. He may have shaken mine as well...I don't remember. He went out and shut the door behind him, and I collapsed into Todd's waiting arms and wept.

The following pages contain the story of my journey from the time I was diagnosed with cancer five years ago until the present. I have included details of my physical, emotional, and spiritual struggles, as well as the intermingled triumphs, as a reminder of God's utter faithfulness regardless of our circumstances.

I have spoken with hundreds of cancer patients, and each and every one of them has a unique story. Please know that only a very small percentage of cancer patients find themselves facing as numerous, severe, traumatic, or persistent challenges as I.

Whether you are reading this book as a newly-diagnosed cancer patient, the loved one of a patient, or are facing some trial or obstacle of a totally different nature, my prayer is that in these pages you find hope, regardless of your situation. I pray you find encouragement to fight your own upcoming battle. And I pray you find comfort as it is portrayed through a relationship with God.

LJM
April 2007

# Chapter One

August in Indiana is usually quite warm and humid. My wedding day on August 1st, 1987, was no exception. For the prior 15 years that I had lived in Indiana, they all were about the same. This particular August of 2002 was no different.

I had just returned from a trip to Texas and was getting our two kids ready to start school. Nate was about to start 7th grade and Courtney was entering 5th. Todd had requested we squeeze in a quick family visit to the State Fair in Indianapolis before the beginning of school.

We got up early and left for Indianapolis, which is about two hours south of the northern Indiana cornfields we call home. Although I didn't feel very good, I didn't want to miss out on the family time. We arrived and began a very long, hot day that involved a lot of walking. I soon began to feel weird – I was nauseous, felt faint, and had severe stomach pain. Somehow I made it until noon, when I was afraid I was going to faint and realized that I just couldn't keep going. Todd got me settled in a chair in a big arena area and brought me a snack. At my suggestion, he and the kids took off for more exploring, but I soon began feeling worse and worse. I became nauseated and dizzy. I had a horrible burning sensation from my throat on down to my ribcage; and, from my ribcage down, I was experiencing what felt like a huge cramp that wouldn't quit. I was so relieved when Todd and the kids came back. Although none of us wanted to cut the day short, it was obvious that I needed to get home to bed.

The next day I went to my doctor, Dr. Nichols, who said I had severe acid reflux disease and put me on Prilosec. Three days later, my throat and ribs stopped burning, but my lower abdomen felt worse than before, and I was still dizzy and nauseous. Dr. Nichols suggested I come back in for a long overdue woman's checkup and, sure enough, she discovered that one of my ovaries had a cyst on it. She assured me that cysts are common and usually drain themselves. But because this one was larger than usual, just to be cautious, she wanted me to go to the hospital for an ultrasound. Her office called the next day and told me that I had an appointment to see a specialist to find out the ultrasound results.

Meanwhile, my belly was growing, and I was losing my appetite as well as significant weight. (Because I have always been rather thin, the weight loss was a concern.) When Todd and I went to see the specialist, he told us that the cyst was the size of a grapefruit, and that it looked like it wasn't going to drain itself. He recommended surgery to remove the affected ovary, but suggested we consider a total hysterectomy to avoid the possibility of needing a second surgery later to remove the other ovary.

Not only was I terribly afraid of the surgery – I couldn't deal with the possibility of having a hysterectomy at age 34. Even though we were done with our biological family, a hysterectomy sounded too drastic.

We asked for input from various family members. My mother, greatly relieved that it wasn't cancer, considered me extremely lucky to have the option of a hysterectomy rather than enduring natural menopause. Todd, Daddy, and my sister Gayle agreed that the hysterectomy was a good option. Knowing my fear of needles, Gayle also concurred with the doctor that having a hysterectomy was preferable to the removal of just one ovary. They all weighed in with their own perspective on my "good news."

Finally, I could stand it no longer. "Have you all lost your minds?!? Don't you understand that the doctor plans to cut me open and take out my organs?!?" I ranted.

My sister Debbie was the one who seemed to appreciate my misgivings and was sympathetic to my plight. She asked when the surgery was scheduled and how I was feeling and what she could do for me. At last someone felt sorry for me! As pathetic as it seems in retrospect, that's exactly what I needed – sympathy.

The surgery was scheduled for the next Wednesday. We had less than a week to make a decision about the hysterectomy idea. By the time Monday rolled around, we had gone back and forth and gotten so many opinions that my head was spinning. Little did I know that the decision would be taken totally out of our hands.

On Monday I needed to go to Dr. Nichols to get all my pre-surgery paperwork and blood work done. My neighbor Lois took me because I could never be trusted to drive after a blood draw – I was known to faint, due to my phobia of needles.

I went into the examination room alone, and the nurse asked me all the important questions, from insurance information to family health history. At one point, she said, "Uh-oh." She went on to say that the specialist I had seen earlier didn't accept my health insurance. She left the room to confer with Dr. Nichols.

After 30 long minutes, Dr. Nichols came in to see me. She said, "Hello, how are you feeling today?" But before I could answer, her eyes fell on my now very large belly and she gasped, "When did this happen? You look five months pregnant!"

I told her that it had grown quickly since I had seen her the previous week, and that I was feeling very faint. She responded that the cyst was taking my blood supply, and that I was not to drive or do anything strenuous before the surgery on Wednesday. She checked me over, and then left the room with a very worried look on her face. (For the record, I had never seen Dr. Nichols shaken-up or frightened. When Courtney was born with the umbilical cord around her neck, Dr. Nichols calmly unwrapped the cord and told me I had a beautiful baby girl. I never knew about the cord until some time later.)

Dr. Nichol's tone of voice, as she talked to the nurses in the hall, was enough to strike great fear into my heart. I overheard her saying that I could not wait another day to see a specialist, and the surgery had to take place soon. The nurse soon returned with an appointment card for me to see a Dr. Sharpe in Lafayette yet that morning. Lois and I left for home. I called Todd to let him know what was going on – the original specialist was not doing the surgery, and I was headed to see a Dr. Sharpe instead. Lois was willing to take me. I assured him that he could stay at work, I'd be fine. I asked him to pray that I could still have the surgery on Wednesday, as originally planned.

Lois and I headed for Lafayette, a city about an hour south of where we live. By this time I knew that my surgery would take place in one of the two large hospitals there, but I had yet to meet my doctor, and the date of surgery was still to be determined.

When we arrived, I filled out a ream of paperwork, and then met alone with Dr. Sharpe. At this point, the cyst thing was huge and the examination very painful. After he was finished and I got dressed, he re-entered the room and sat down with a grave look on his face.

"Lori," he said, "This thing is not a cyst, it is a tumor. It is so wrapped around your ovaries, that I recommend a total hysterectomy." He then asked, "Do you have any history of cancer in your family?"

I was ready for his comments, but the cancer question totally threw me. My mind struggled to focus as fear was working its way up my throat and threatening to strangle my words.

"My grandpa on my dad's side died from pancreatic cancer when he was 76," I answered. "No one else in my family has had cancer. Why are you asking me this? And what is the difference between a cyst and a tumor?"

"A cyst is fluid-filled. It is never cancerous, and it can sometimes drain itself without surgery. A tumor is a mass of tissue that may or may not be cancerous. There is a slight possibility that your tumor is cancerous. Are you sure no one else has had cancer in your family?"

"I am sure. So you are telling me I might have cancer?" I asked with a shaky voice.

"The odds are that you don't have cancer, especially with your family history. But I want to be straightforward: there is a possibility that you have cancer. Again, your odds of having cancer are very low, and there is no need to worry. Now, when would you like to have the surgery?"

I requested Wednesday, as I had already told my friends and family that's when it would be. He said he'd see what he could do. The date of surgery depended on availability of an operating room.

A few minutes later his nurse came in and said my surgery was scheduled for Friday at 8:00 A.M. She apologized that she was unable to secure an operating room for Wednesday. I thanked her, got my blood work orders, and left.

That night as I lay in bed, I was surrounded by fear that gripped me so tightly I could hardly pray. Todd gently reassured me. "Let's not worry about the 'maybe,' let's just face what we know and go from there." But I detected a hint of fear in his voice. I cried myself to sleep as Todd held me close.

The next morning Todd and I drove two hours north to a city on the outskirts of Chicago, where we were scheduled to be fingerprinted by the FBI. This was one of the final steps to complete our paperwork for adopting a child from China. According to our adoption agency, we would have our baby by December.

I recall thinking that our two worlds weren't lining up. On the one hand, we eagerly awaited the arrival of a child who had been birthed in our hearts by God. On the other, the symptoms of my tumor were making me feel increasingly faint and tired, and I was scheduled for major surgery in a few days. I tried to take comfort in the words of Scripture, "God's ways are not our ways, His thoughts are not our thoughts." i

Having finished the fingerprinting, which took a mere 20 minutes, we stopped at K-Mart© to get some pajamas for my hospital stay. As we approached the checkout line, I began to feel wobbly and light-headed. I told Todd I needed fresh air and started to the truck, leaving him to check out. As I stepped outside, the sound of ocean waves began to throb in my head and my vision went blurry. I fixed my gaze on the truck and headed for it as fast as my wobbly legs would carry me. I was in a race against time: I knew I was about to go down. I just needed to get to the truck...

My next memory is of Todd gently trying to get me into the truck. Coming out of the store and seeing me about to "bite the dust," he sprinted across the parking lot and reached me just as I fell. Thank God he was there to catch me!

As I settled into bed that night, I prayed Friday would come quickly, and that I wouldn't faint again before then. Todd lay beside me, stroking my arm. I remember well the worried look on his face. I assured him that the surgery would soon be over and I would be fine. On the next day, Wednesday, I was going to do nothing but rest. That was the plan.

But Wednesday didn't get that memo...

# Chapter Two

The minute I woke up, I knew something was wrong. I had extremely sharp pains in my abdomen. I was afraid to move. If it hurt this much just to lie here, how much worse would it be if I tried to move? I looked at the clock. 5:30 A.M. Todd should still be downstairs, getting ready for work. I needed to get to him before he left.

My mind overruled my body's pain, and I slowly rolled to my side and attempted to sit up. But a piercing pain doubled me over, bringing tears to my eyes. I rolled to the floor and lay there, gasping for breath and trying to remember what I had learned in breathing class to prepare me for childbirth. It wasn't working. I began a painful half-crawl, half-slither across the bedroom floor. If I could only get to the hall and yell for Todd before he left! I knew I was going to faint, but I couldn't! I had no choice but to get to the hall.

I only made it to the doorway of our room before rolling into a fetal position to try to keep from fainting. With all the strength I could muster, I groaned, "T-o-d-d!!!"

I heard his footsteps quickly approaching. He was taking the stairs two at a time. Taking one look at me, his face paled. He immediately took charge: he would call a neighbor to come for the kids and he would take me to the emergency room. As he ran back down the stairs, mingled with my pain was a sense of relief. I had gotten to him in time. Thank You, God!

The next thing I felt was a small, cool hand on my forehead, and I heard Courtney's fear-laced voice, "Mommy, are you all right? What's wrong?"

"M-o-m-m-y i-s j-u-s-t h-a-v-i-n-g s-o-m-e p-a-i-n," I croaked. "I w-i-l-l b-e a-l-l r-i-g-h-t. P-l-e-a-s-e t-r-y t-o b-e b-r-a-v-e f-o-r M-o-m-m-y."

She was gone for just an instant before she returned with a pillow, a blanket, and a stuffed bear. Although it was unbelievably hard to lift my head for her to put the pillow under it, somehow I managed. The teddy bear was a welcome gift – I squeezed it tightly to redirect my pain.

Todd returned and, seeing Courtney's great concern, assured her I was going to be okay and told her Lois was on the way. As Todd helped me get dressed, Courtney worriedly looked on; I tried to stifle my sobs. Todd helped me into one of his t-shirts and a pair of sweat pants that were large enough to accommodate my large belly. Noticing my bare feet, he ran to my drawer, pulled out the first pair of socks he could find – white with pink pigs – and put them on me. He then ran outside to get the car, while Courtney sat with me and stroked my head. How well I remember the sweet sound of her voice as she prayed over me.

When Lois arrived, just a few minutes later, Todd gently scooped me up and carried me to the car. Courtney handed me the bear again, and the last thing I saw as we pulled away was her collapsing in tears into Lois' arms.

Todd punched the accelerator and we were off. (We really found out what was under the hood of that pink Cadillac!) A trip that usually takes an hour took us 35 minutes that morning. Doubled over in pain, I clung to the bear and the door handle in turn. Todd, who often talks to himself, was begging for an officer to come and stop us, so we would have a police escort to the hospital. Where are those policemen when you need them?

Lois had called ahead, and the hospital staff met us at the door with a wheelchair. Soon I was on a gurney – clammy, dizzy, nauseous, and in extreme pain. I wept as they started an IV. As bad as the belly pain, my fear of needles was almost worse.

Once the pain was under control, I was taken for tests. Then we waited for Dr. Sharpe. When he came in there was no time for discussion or explanation. The tumor had burst, and I was heading into emergency surgery within 20 minutes. The doctor went to scrub, and the nurses wheeled me into the holding area to wait my turn. The anesthesiologist came in, introduced himself, and explained what he was going to do. Dr. Sharpe came in and announced that we were ready to go. Then he quipped, "Lori, you really did want this surgery on Wednesday, didn't you?"

Todd asked if we could pray. To my surprise, the two doctors took our hands and, along with Todd, circled my bed. Todd committed my life into their expert hands and, ultimately, into God's. Then they left. I was so scared – I can't begin to explain what was going on in my heart and mind. I saw raw fear in Todd's eyes. We held each other tightly and sobbed until they came for me.

I have said good-bye to Todd many times, but none was as difficult as that good-bye. It was so uncertain; so hard. We didn't know if I would survive, or was this our final goodbye. We just didn't know. We had to trust that God was in control, but we sure wished we could foresee the outcome.

I don't watch many hospital-type shows on television, but, from the few I had seen, I remember what an operating room looked like. "This is just like on television," I said as I was wheeled in. I could see the eyes of several of the assisting technicians crinkle in smiles. I looked around at a roomful of eight or so blue-clad people – they all looked like 'Smurfs'. I said as much; again, the crinkly smiles. The anesthesiologist then came to my side and told me to begin to count backwards from 100. I got to ninety.

Meanwhile, Todd was joined in the waiting room by his Dad and sister Tammy. Then in came my Mom, Daddy, and my sister Debbie. A friend from church and our pastor joined them. They waited. They talked. They prayed. And they waited some more. As they were about to go get something to eat, they saw a girl being wheeled into surgery to have her tonsils removed. On the way back from the cafeteria, they saw her being taken to her room. Todd commented that she must have had a hard time of it – she looked terrible! Then his eyes fell on her socks – white background with little pink pigs. I looked so pitiful that he hadn't even recognized his own wife! He broke down and wept.

My next memory is one I would rather forget. I was in a fog from the anesthetic, but absolutely incredible pain pierced through the fog. The nurse assured me I'd get some pain relief when I got to my room. I was convinced that couldn't happen soon enough.

Finally, the gurney was rolling toward my room. Every bump, every corner, and every tile on the floor was excruciating. As the nurses grabbed the ends of my sheet and hefted me up and over, the pain was once again unbelievable. Would it never end?

Todd was then allowed to come into the room. I saw his loving face, streaked with tears. Somehow it seemed he had more worry lines and gray hairs than just a few hours previously. Bless his heart – how hard the waiting must have been! He came to my side, held my hand, and bent down to kiss my face. As he did so, I squeezed his hand with all my might and said, in no uncertain terms, "Get me some pain relief!" It wasn't soon enough, but relief finally came.

I later learned why I had so much pain after the surgery. In a scheduled surgery, the anesthesiologist first inserts an epidural into the patient's lower back. When the patient wakes up after surgery, the epidural has kicked in, providing adequate pain relief until the morphine pump is hooked up. In an emergency situation such as mine, however, the surgeon goes first, then the anesthesiologist. When I woke up, the epidural hadn't had adequate time to work, so I had no pain relief in my system. Consequently, I felt as if I had been cut open and filleted.

The surgeon had removed a tumor the size of a football, as well as all of my female organs. He had also removed some lymph nodes to send to pathology.

"Do I have cancer?" I asked Todd.

"We won't know until the report comes back from pathology – possibly in a week or so. Right now, let's just concentrate on getting you strong enough to get out of here!"

There were several precursors to my leaving the hospital. I had to be weaned off the IV morphine, and put onto oral medicine. I had to be able to walk on my own. I had to use the restroom. I had to have no infection or fever. Todd looked over the list and approached it like a drill sergeant.

The day after my surgery, after a sleepless night for both Todd and me, the nurse came in and announced that I was going to get up and walk. In spite of my looking at her as if she was crazy, she proceeded to get all my tubes and wires organized, and she and Todd helped me sit up. I protested. There was no way I could walk. They both insisted otherwise. So I began to walk; Todd supported me on one side with the nurse on the other, while tubes and wires trailed along behind. We made it to the door before I fainted into Todd's arms.

Recovery was slow and painful, but ten days after surgery I was discharged from the hospital. We were back to see Dr. Sharpe and get the staples removed a week later. Although the nurse had assured me that it "wouldn't hurt a bit," the procedure was extremely painful for me. After she had finished and left the room, Dr. Sharpe came in to check me. He said again the surgery had been successful; they had gotten the whole tumor. Next came the words I will never, ever forget: "You have cancer."

"You have cancer." The words echoed off the walls of the doctor's office like the sound of a metal ball in a pinball machine spinning out of control. My world began to spin just as wildly. I know the doctor kept talking. "Stage 2 ovarian cancer. We're lucky to have caught it in this early stage."

"We recommend six months of chemotherapy."

"I have referred you to a doctor. He would like to see you as soon as possible." I am so glad Todd was there and actually paying attention. My world was whirling. I was unsuccessfully trying to wrap my mind around those three simple yet potentially life-shattering words, "You have cancer."

Dr. Sharpe got up from his chair and moved to shake Todd's hand. He may have shaken mine as well...I don't remember. He went out and shut the door behind him, and I collapsed into Todd's waiting arms, and wept.

# Chapter Three

We left the doctor's office in a blur. My mother, who had accompanied us, was waiting in the lobby. Too stunned to speak, I sat quietly beside her as Todd completed the paperwork. Once the three of us were in the car, I burst into tears, and Todd managed to tell my mother what the doctor had said. She held together well initially, but, when she called Daddy to tell him the news, the tears began to flow.

Mom, Todd, and I were trying to get a grip on reality and yet be strong for each other. It was surreal...so weird...and new and different and uncertain and scary. The trip home was characterized by statements of total disbelief intermingled with long moments of shocked silence.

Finally, I asked, "How are we going to tell the kids?" I had absolutely no concept of how to break news such as this to our children.

We developed a plan of action. We would call our church, our family, and some friends, telling them what was happening and requesting their prayers for our family. Then, when the kids got home from school, we would tell it to them straight.

That is exactly how it went down. Just as we finished telling the kids, our pastor arrived. Courtney was on Grandma's lap, both of them crying. I was on the living room couch, sobbing as I witnessed Courtney's response to the devastating news. Todd, who had spent most of his time answering the phone since we had arrived home, came into the living room to join Pastor Jeff, mom, Courtney and me. Pastor Jeff shared some comforting verses from the Bible, and we talked and cried and prayed together.

And then there was Nate. He wandered aimlessly from room to room, finally ending up outside. He was so obviously trying to escape an inescapable pain. The raw truth was his mom had cancer, and he didn't know what to do with that. Throughout the next several months, he curled himself up into an emotional cocoon, and there he stayed. He wore a tough guy exterior, telling whoever asked that his mom was fine, he was fine, everything was fine. We were worried about him.

Courtney, by contrast, wore her heart on her sleeve. The ten days I was gone for the surgery had been torture for her. What now? Was this going to take me away from her again? She cried openly and often. We never wondered what she was thinking and feeling. She had assumed the role of nurse while I was recovering from the hysterectomy, and she immediately thrust herself back into a caregiving role. Keeping busy seemed to somehow lessen her fear.

The next week was a flurry of activity. We made the 100-mile round trip to Lafayette every day. On Monday Todd and I met with the oncologist, Dr. Hanse, a kind, soft-spoken man. His large, deep brown eyes swam with compassion, and his bedside manner was A+. He told us again that even though the surgeon had removed the whole tumor, there were likely cancer cells floating around in my body. The cancerous tumor had burst inside me. We needed to attack those cells with chemotherapy, which would destroy the cancer cells. Unfortunately, good cells would be destroyed as well, accounting for the side effects. He said that on Wednesday the nurse would go through all that with me.

My diagnosis was Stage 2 Ovarian Cancer. We were told that ovarian cancer is most often caught in stage 3 or 4, and by then the prognosis is not good. Mine was caught early, so the prognosis was good. However, the doctor said it was imperative to start the chemo as soon as possible. Did we have any questions for him?

"Yes. Am I going to lose my hair?" I asked.

"I'm sorry, but yes, you are. The chemo that is prescribed for ovarian cancer is strong, and one of the side effects is hair loss."

"Is there some way that we could get those floating cancer cells without me losing my hair? What about radiation? Would that kill the cancer without killing my hair follicles?" With each subsequent question I was nearer to full-blown panic.

"I'm sorry, no. Radiation is a targeted form of cancer treatment that goes only to the affected areas. Because we don't know where the cancer cells are, we must use chemo that will go throughout your body and enter every cell."

"I'm not okay with this. Todd, I can't lose my hair. Todd, no... ." Although in my head I knew there was no other option, my emotions were far from ready to accept the inevitable. I cried myself to sleep that night.

On Tuesday, Mom and I went to meet the "wig lady." She took pictures of me from the front, back, and sides, snipped a piece of my hair so she could match the color, and measured my head. Then we began to discuss my wig options. The synthetic one was cheaper, but would melt if I got too close to an oven or flame. The real hair one was very expensive, but it would last much longer and would look like my own hair. Or, I could forget the wig and opt for a bandana or hat. I went with the real hair. I didn't want anyone to know that I was losing my hair. This was such an incredibly sensitive issue to me!

On Wednesday, Mom and I returned to Dr. Hanse's office to receive pre-chemo instructions. Sally, the nurse, explained all sorts of things to us that day – including the only thing that I could remember later: every chemo treatment was given through an IV line. I wanted to bolt. Sally said they had heard about my needle phobia, and that the doctors had agreed that a port, surgically implanted under my skin just below the collarbone, would be a great option for me. The port would allow needles to be inserted, medicine administered, and blood drawn without accessing veins. Could they schedule an appointment to implant the device? Mom said yes. Surgically implanting the port, followed by chemotherapy, was scheduled for the next day. From my vantage point, things were moving way too quickly. But Dr. Hanse was in a hurry to destroy the traveling cancer cells before they set up shop in a major organ.

As we left the doctor's office, I was again in tears. My mom was a rock and so very patient with me. When we got home she gave Todd details of our doctor's visit. She shared with us both – since I really wasn't listening to Sally – the list of potential side effects from chemo: vomiting, dehydration, nausea, weight loss, hair loss, lowered resistance to disease, allergic reaction, dizziness, fatigue, diarrhea, mouth sores, and head sores. I was scared. So was my family.

The following morning, Todd and I arrived at the hospital for insertion of the port. I donned the lovely hospital gown and the nurse came in to insert an IV to get the fluids going. After three agonizing tries, and me nearly fainting in the process, she got the needle in.

We sat in a holding area until Dr. Oliver came in and introduced himself. He talked really fast, and the only part I caught was that I would not be totally unconscious for the procedure. They would have me "loopy" enough that I wouldn't feel it or remember it, but I would be awake. I begged him to knock me out! He said that would require rescheduling the surgery, because I would need to stay overnight and have an anesthesiologist. I told him to proceed, because I was not coming back to get pricked again! He left to scrub.

Meanwhile, I had noticed that there was a big, purple bump growing where the IV was inserted. When the nurse returned to check on me, she said "Oh, no!" and hurriedly left the room.

I looked at Todd and said, "No way! Tell me this one is going to work – I can't go through another IV insertion!" He held my hand as another nurse appeared and said, "I'm sorry, Lori. We have to try again on that IV. I'll do the best I can and pray that we get it on the first try."

I am usually a very friendly, outgoing person. But at this juncture, I'll admit, I was not a ray of sunshine! I just sat there and buried my head in Todd's arm and sobbed so hard I barely felt the prick. Thank

God, this one worked!

When they got me back to the now-familiar operating room, one of the assisting technicians looked at me and said, “I know you! You are the seven pound tumor! I held that thing in a pan! It was unbelievable! How are you doing?”

I had to chuckle a little. How did she recognize me? The last time she saw me I was headed to emergency surgery: no make-up, a whitewashed face, and totally flat hair. This time, I had on make-up, there was color in my cheeks, and my hair was curled! “Yes, I was the ‘seven pound tumor.’ But how on earth did you recognize me?”

“Your nails,” she responded. “They are long with French tips. I couldn’t easily forget that!”

Another nurse looked at me then and said, “Aren’t you the Mary Kay lady?”

“Yes,” I answered, intrigued that these people knew me.

“I lost my consultant and need some lipstick. Can I order that from you?” she continued.

I made a mental note of her order for two lipsticks before they began to insert the pain meds and the anesthetic through my IV. I was rather groggy but we were visiting a little. Dr. Oliver was moving along with the surgery, and all was going well. Then I heard a distinct “Scalpel, please.”

I jumped. It’s one thing to know that they were going to cut on me and quite another to know the cutting was imminent! Thankfully, they gave me more anesthetic as they continued to insert the port. I was greatly relieved when the procedure was done.

After thirty minutes in recovery, the nurse came in to take out the IV. I stopped her in her tracks. Knowing the next procedure would involve inserting dye in my veins via IV, I asked, “Can we keep the IV? We are heading from here to get a Computed Tomography (CT) scan and I really don’t want to have to have another one inserted.” She readily agreed. After our traumatic beginning, she was not about to make me go through that again. God bless her.

We walked across the way to the CT building, where I was quickly whisked away to don yet another lovely gown. They brought me a large cup of barium and I tried to force down the nasty-tasting stuff.

Then, to my great surprise, in walked my sister Debbie and her fiancé, Mark. How they found us, I will never know! Having Debbie there gave Todd a welcome break from helping me don hospital gowns, and coaxing me to drink barium. When they took me away for the CT, Todd had some company. Thank you, God, for orchestrating this on our behalf.

After the preparation, the CT itself was anticlimactic. I just laid there while they put me through this tunnel-like tube and took pictures.

It had been a long day. I was half drugged, worn to a frazzle, and I just wanted to crawl in bed. Tomorrow was going to be another big day.

I was starting chemotherapy.

# Chapter Four

A general who is preparing to wage war against the enemy needs a strategic plan of action. Strong leadership and clear direction is imperative to make wise decisions about placement of troops, attacks, counterattacks, fortification, and reconnaissance. Strategy is determined by the specifics of the war being waged. In World War I, combat was face-to-face. The airplane was introduced for battle in World War II. By Desert Storm in the 90's, fighter jet pilots were given exact coordinates so the "smart bomb" could be dropped with precision.

I had no concept of what it would be like to begin treatment to eradicate the cancer from my body. I felt as if I was caught in the midst of a war for which I hadn't volunteered. The battleground: my body. The weaponry: chemotherapy. The problem: the whereabouts of the enemy, cancer – if, in fact, it existed at all – was totally unknown.

We checked in with Dr. Hanse on that Friday morning and then waited. I was afraid. This whole day would begin with a relentless phobia – a needle prick right into my port! Two nurses came in.

They explained what they were going to do, and then started the procedure. As one of them accessed the port I cried and squeezed Todd's hand. The needle was in.

Both nurses stayed in my cubicle, watching me closely and checking vital signs often. First, a bag of saline fluid began to drip into my body. Next was a 20-minute drip of Benadryl©, in case I had an allergic reaction, followed by an anti-nausea drug. Finally, the first bag of chemo began to flow into my body.

When I was finished, the nurses gave me some oral anti-nausea medication and instructed me to call if I had a fever, rash, excessive vomiting, or any unusual reactions. Diarrhea was to be expected, and they explained that what would be coming out of me would be toxic, and could harm my family, so we needed to take precautions. If this stuff was so toxic after it had filtered through my body, I could only imagine what it was doing inside me!

I slept a lot on Saturday. Although I felt weird inside, I was not sick or dizzy or nauseated, and I ate normally. But on Sunday everything changed. With no warning, I became very sick. I rushed to the bathroom, lost everything in my stomach, and returned to the couch. I took all the anti-nausea stuff I could. Nothing helped. I felt like I was on a roller coaster that was doing "loop-de-loops." Oh, how I wanted to get off! I had a sleepless night, getting up countless times to throw up. I felt wretched!

When Monday morning arrived, it was clear I needed someone to help me while Todd was at work. He first called my mom. Although she hated to say "no," she recognized that she was emotionally and physically spent. She was on the verge of a breakdown and knew she would be no good to me like that. I understood.

My mom had been on the front lines since day one. She nursed me back to health after my surgery, was alongside when we heard the word "cancer," and had taken me for numerous medical appointments. She drove carpools for the children's activities, put meals on the table, washed the dishes, cleaned the house, and did the laundry. She helped the kids with homework, and held Courtney as she wept. She did these labors of love even as she was trying to wrap her mind around the fact that her daughter had cancer. Now she needed Daddy. She needed to be home for a while and regain some sense of normalcy, because what was going on around our house could not, by any stretch of the imagination, be considered as such.

Todd had missed so many days of work. He knew he really needed to go in, but he also knew he couldn't leave me alone. He called our neighbor Lois, who once again graciously agreed to help. Within five minutes she was at our house.

Lois had a very sick patient on her hands. I could barely get out of bed. The world would not stop spinning. I couldn't stand any noise, and any sort of smell made me even more nauseous. I felt like I had the worst imaginable case of food poisoning. I was afraid I was going to die. Then I wished I would.

Time stood still. I would sing songs in my head and then look at the clock and realize only two minutes had passed. I tried to envision what I would do when I felt better. I sang more songs. I recited all the scripture verses I could remember. I mentally wrote a testimony that I would share if I lived, and if I ever could stand upright again and go to church. I prayed and prayed and prayed some more. Then I looked at the clock. Twenty minutes had passed.

Lois made chicken broth, and lovingly and quietly, every hour on the hour, she would bring me some. The smell alone made my stomach swirl. I lay there, more miserable than I had ever been, and I prayed and cried out to God! Was I going to feel this horrible for the next six months of chemo? With time standing still and my misery mounting, I selfishly prayed for God to take me to heaven. He didn't. I prayed some more. I lived on. I had a choice: I drink the broth and give myself a fighting chance of survival, or I don't drink the broth and eventually die of starvation. I thought long and hard.

I have never had suicidal tendencies – this struggle was the product of an abused body, and a despairing mind. I thought about Nate and Courtney and Todd. I thought about Jenna, our "China doll" who was still a world away, but scheduled to arrive in our home in four months. I thought about my parents and my siblings. I thought about my friends. I decided to at least do my part and try to live. Then, if God called me to heaven, it was His decision, not mine.

I rolled over and slowly, painfully, spoonful by spoonful, drank the broth. It came back up. Lois brought more and I tried again. And again. And again. It finally stayed down. By Tuesday, I was able to add a few crackers. Still not able to move around, I lay in my quiet, lonely little bedroom. Wednesday, although weak and wobbly, I was able to sit up in bed for ten minutes before I collapsed, exhausted. By the end of that week, I was able to keep down crackers and broth, and finally, with Todd's help, I ventured downstairs to my family and the "land of the living." For the next two weeks I continued to be nauseous. Although I realized that I wouldn't feel this bad for the whole six months of chemo, I began to dread going back for another round. Soon I began to get sores on my head and in my mouth. Food started to taste like chemicals. I had to eat all natural foods; some simply tasted bland while others tasted bitter.

My hair began to fall out. Everywhere. I called my dear friend Ericka and asked her to take me to get my wig. She readily agreed. It was my first venture outside of our yard in two weeks. My wig was ready as promised. The wig lady was going to shave my head, but I wasn't brave enough for that. I decided to just let it continue to fall out, and to wear the wig as soon as I needed to. In addition to the wig of real hair, we chose a night hat and a synthetic wig to wear around the house. A group of ladies from a church in our community had given me some money, and I was praying that it would be enough to pay for everything. The wig lady bagged it all up and said, "No charge."

What? She explained that someone who asked to remain anonymous had called ahead and said to put whatever I purchased that day on his or her credit card. Although we tried, we never found out the identity of this person who touched my life in such a caring and unassuming way. Only three people even knew that I was getting a wig, and I had told no one from whom it was going to be purchased. Each of them denied being the benefactor. Who knew God has a credit card!

Ericka helped me put the wig on and we headed home. Todd and the kids were in the yard tossing a football around when we pulled into the yard. Courtney was the first one to the car. Her reaction: "Mommy, I thought you were going to get a wig!" Nate was next. He simply said, "Did you change your mind about your wig?" Finally, Todd came to help me out of the car. He asked if I brought the wig home.

I looked at Ericka, and we began to chuckle. Then we told them all that I had the wig on. They could hardly believe it! I truly thought that Todd had "prepped" the kids so I would feel more comfortable, but he hadn't. The wig looked just like my own hair. I was so grateful to God! One thing in my life could at least look normal. That night I fell asleep praising God for small miracles, and slept more soundly than I had for many nights.

Having a wig that looked like my own hair seems like such an insignificant thing in light of all I was facing, but, as much as possible for the sake of my family, I wanted life to go on as usual. This was one small step in that direction. That being settled, God and I had some other matters to address. But that wasn't to happen until after my second round of chemo.

God had something else in mind...

# Chapter Five

I was able to go to church one time between my first two chemo treatments. I was weak in body, but sustained in spirit as I was surrounded by dear friends who had been doing so much for us – praying, bringing in meals, cleaning our home, leaving gift baskets on our doorstep, sending notes of encouragement, and helping us financially. They, too, were encouraged to see me in person, after many weeks of worrying and wondering.

Hoping I would be able to go to church, I had called Pastor Jeff and asked if I could share a testimony. What I hadn't considered at the time I called him, however, was that I was going to be completely bald by Sunday. I would be sharing my testimony the same day I was debuting my new wig. As I sat in the pew, I began to feel very apprehensive. What if everybody noticed my wig? What if it slid to the side, or worse yet, fell off? Or, my wig concerns aside, what if I wasn't strong enough to walk to the front of the sanctuary and speak? As I was beginning to regret my decision to share my testimony, Pastor Jeff said my name. So much for escaping! I got up gingerly and headed toward the pulpit, praying for strength with each step.

God gave me strength, and so much more. He gave me a sense of purpose, and a sense of destiny. This cancer was what He had allowed into my life, and He had promised to walk with me through every stage of it. That meant He was with me on this day too. As I began to speak, I felt stronger, not weaker! This is what I shared.

> Coming to terms with my diagnosis of cancer has been an emotional journey with many stages. I would like to share them with you.
>
> Stage one was denial. The "this can't be happening to me" syndrome. I went from shock to disbelief to anger to self-pity. I kept asking, "Why me?!" There is something surreal about being told you have a disease that threatens your very life, and whose cure is almost as devastating as the disease itself. It is also very sobering, and causes your perspective to change.
>
> Stage two found me better able to grasp reality. When you are actually thrust into chemotherapy, and you are living with the side effects and the fear, you really get a grip. My second stage led me to ask "Why not me?" rather than "Why me?" We live in a sinful world where evil and disease abounds. Why should I be immune to the effects of it? I am not promised anywhere in God's Word that I will not suffer pain and hardship but, rather, I am promised that if I live godly in Christ Jesus, I will suffer persecution.
>
> This led me to stage three and the hardest one so far that I have had to grapple with. God was not taken by surprise by my diagnosis. (Sure, we were sideswiped!!) He

didn't look down from His throne one day and say, "Oops! How did that one slip by Me?" Rather, He knew – He planned from the time I was born, that when I turned 34 years, 2 months and 15 days old I would be struck with cancer. He has been in control the whole time and has not lost His grip! But I had! I was still questioning the point of the whole thing and actually arguing with God over the wisdom of it. That led to a very real wrestling match I had early one morning. I knew what God was nudging me to do as I lay there in bed, but in my stubbornness I refused to "let go and let God." We went back and forth for quite awhile, God and I, until finally, exhausted and crying, I was able to actually thank Him for this disease. That released me to see more clearly His purpose for me. We are told in Corinthians, James, Hebrews, and many other places that the trials He brings into our lives are to mature us and better us and to make us more like Himself. How could I not be thankful for THAT? I now am actually looking forward to the life lessons He has wrapped inside this disease. I want to grow to know Him better, and to be able to be a stronger, more mature vessel for Him to work through. I can only begin to imagine the greater sense of empathy that I will have with those He brings into my path who are themselves suffering. What a gift this really is!

Okay...I am still scared. I am scared of the pain and the nausea, and the discomfort. I am afraid of the unknowns and the uncertainties. I don't relish the journey I have to take over the next several months. I don't know what the future holds, but I am resting confidently in the care of the One who holds the future.

LJM
October, 2002

I returned to my seat with a renewed sense of hope. God had given me the strength to share my story for His glory.

Debbie and Mark had agreed to take me for my next chemo appointment. Dr. Hanse told me that my white cell count had been quite low from the last round, so that needed to be checked before we could go ahead with the chemo. Then he sat down in his chair and rolled it up close to mine.

"Lori, I promised you from the start that I would be straightforward with you about your prognosis and how everything is going. This is your body. These are your test results. You deserve to know what is going on." I reached for Debbie's hand. She squeezed it reassuringly.

Dr. Hanse continued, "One of your tests came back from pathology showing a cell that looks like colon cancer. It was only one report out of all your results. The tests are wrong often enough that, given how unusual this would be, I am relatively sure there is no colon cancer."

I was confused. "I thought I have ovarian cancer. How could colon cancer be in my ovary?" I asked.

"That's just it. Usually, cancer travels through the lymph nodes, but in your case there was no sign of cancer in them. So the cancer cells would have had to travel through your blood stream from your colon to your ovary –bypassing the heart, liver, lungs, kidneys and pancreas. The likelihood of that happening is so slim it isn't even in the textbooks. I feel that we should continue to battle the ovarian cancer, and then later – when you are through with chemo and feeling better – we might send you for a colonoscopy, just to be on the safe side."

"Why aren't we just resting assured that no matter what kind of cancer is in there, the chemo will take care of it?" I asked.

That's when his explanation got much too technical for me. In layman's terms, one type of cancer is unlikely to be destroyed with the chemo prescribed for another. The chemo I was taking for ovarian cancer was seldom effective in eradicating other types. Dr. Hanse felt we should finish the course we had started for the cancer we knew I had. There was always a possibility that it would take care of any other cancer (if it was even there).

He suggested I put this new information in a box and label it to be opened in February or March when we were through with chemo. I could deal with it then. But he assured me again that he felt this was nothing of concern; he just wanted me to be "in the know."

We thanked him, and he went to get a nurse to access my port. If my white cell count was high enough, we would proceed with the chemo as scheduled. As for the new information, we would, as the doctor had suggested, "box it up" until next year.

After they drew blood we had an hour to kill before the results would be back from the lab. Mark asked if there were anything special that I would like to do. Without hesitation, I answered, "Yes! I ɔ 'normal people stuff'!"

ʌw do you define that?" he asked.

I knew just the thing. I am a sucker for the puppies in the mall, and I wanted to go see them. As I believe God had planned it especially for me, a breeder was bringing in a litter of Pekingese puppies just as we arrived. They hadn't been put in the cages yet; we literally took them from the breeder's arms. They had that awesome "puppy smell," and because they were scared of their new environment, they lay still in our arms.

Debbie and I were enjoying every moment. We grew up with a Pekingese dog named Benji, and memories were flooding back. I named one of the puppies Spunky. The pet shop worker saw that I obviously had fallen for Spunky and suggested I take him home with me. I explained that I had recently been diagnosed with ovarian cancer and had come for "puppy therapy" before having a chemotherapy treatment. "Thank you so much for letting me borrow your puppy! It did my heart good!"

I didn't want to leave Spunky and this invigorating, if momentary, escape from reality. The worker was so very kind and sympathetic, telling me to come back any time. The puppies were there at my "cuddle disposal." I ended up going to see Spunky each time I went for blood draws or chemo for the next many, many weeks. When I walked in the door, the lady working there would always bring me "my puppy" and tell me I could take as long as I wanted. I enjoyed Spunky right up through my last round of chemo! Soon after my visits ended, he was sold and left the pet shop with his new owner.

At the end of that first visit to the pet shop, I was ready to face the results of the blood work. We got back to the hospital just as Dr. Hanse received those results. It was a "go." I got settled into my chair in what I began to call my cubicle, and, because they had left the needle in, I just sat back and waited for them to start the Benadryl©.

The treatment was uneventful and took only three hours instead of almost six, as the first one had. Debbie was at my beck and call... even though for most of the time I was out of it. Mark roamed the city of Lafayette looking for a muffin without artificial ingredients so I would have some nourishment. I was very touched by his kindness!

Todd and I had a long talk that night about the possible colon cancer diagnosis. Todd, in his usual manner, suggested that we deal with what we know, and put the unknown on the back burner.

Within a couple of days, the chemo side effects began to once again appear. I needed all the prayer I could get and all the strength I could muster in the next few days!!

# Chapter Six

The potential side effects of chemo I had been told about were simply overwhelming. The list included hair loss, neuropathy, nutropenia, vomiting, diarrhea, dehydration, weight loss, dizziness, fatigue, mouth sores, and head sores.

For whatever reason, I had experienced not just one or two of these side effects, but every one on the list. Plus, I had learned some surprising things. For example, losing my hair hurt. Not just the emotional pain and loss of dignity, but true, physical pain. As I lost every hair on my body, I experienced itching for a couple of days, and then pain as if I had severe sunburn. Aside from the discomfort of pulling a wig over my "sunburned" head, my scalp was full of canker-like sores. Scratching, an instinctive response to itching, caused profuse bleeding. I was trying hard to keep a positive attitude as I worked through some of the very real issues caused by these side effects.

With the second round of chemo, all of these symptoms become more acute. What's more, I seemed to have invented some of my own side effects, new to even my nurses and doctor. These includ-

loss, muscle tension, nerve loss, anxiety, hyperventila-
ng spells, and bruising.

My memory loss was frustrating for our whole family. I would ask Courtney three times in a row to go brush her teeth, even though she had already brushed them and had told me as much. I forgot phone conversations, and could not be trusted with messages. I lost track of what day it was. I forgot where I put things, which round of chemo I was on, and the names of people I had just met. I even forgot where I had put notes to remind myself of things so I wouldn't forget them.

We could have cried about one more thing that cancer had taken from me, but as a family, we decided to laugh instead. I provided many opportunities for laughter! (I'd share them with you, if I could remember them.)

The muscle tension and nerve damage were hard to deal with. After that second round of chemo, I was relaxing on the couch, waiting for the exact 48 hour point at which I would become nauseous when, without warning, my shoulders and neck became tense, throwing my head back. I couldn't return it to a normal position, even with my hands. Todd massaged my shoulders and neck, but nothing helped. Soon the muscle tension was causing intense pain in my back and shoulders. We called the doctor, who said we should go to the emergency room immediately. After an hour's drive and another hour's wait, I was in incredible pain. Only after I was given Valium© did the muscles relax and the pain lessen.

I was home from the emergency room just in time for the other side effects to kick in. I was just as sick as I had been before, and drinking even a spoonful of broth was a struggle. Again I lay in my lonely bedroom, unable to hear sounds or smell smells, unable to move or think straight, with my whole world spinning around me. Again I prayed and sang songs in my head and recited scriptures. And again, time seemed to stand still.

After two weeks of flu-like symptoms, there was a short period of time during which I was able to get out of bed, dress, and go somewhere, like across the yard to my office. An hour later I would go back home and collapse for the rest of the day.

After trial and error, pushing myself too hard and paying for it later, my life during chemo became somewhat of a routine. Life seemed to go on for everyone else; I, by contrast, was not much more than a passive observer.

Nate grew a full 12 inches. Courtney struggled with a demanding teacher and a difficult year academically that translated into three hours of homework every night. Todd advanced in his career as a welder. The adoption proceeded; the time we would get our little Jenna was approaching. I made it to one of Nate's football games, to a Mary Kay meeting once a month, and to church every 3rd week, right before I would have another treatment. The next two treatments were as brutal on my body and emotions as the first two.

In the midst of my chemo-dominated life, Pastor Jeff asked me to write a list of what I was thankful for so he could put it into the bulletin for the Thanksgiving service. Here's what I wrote:

## GS I AM GRATEFUL FOR THIS THANKSGIVING

am grateful I had a tumor that grew so aggressively it sted the attention of doctors and specialists alike.

I am grateful that when I fainted in the parking lot, Todd caught me.

I am grateful my first specialist was unable to take my case and God led us to my second specialist – who, I believe, saved my life.

I am grateful that when the tumor burst, Todd hadn't yet left for work.

I am grateful that, since we had to go into the E. R., we have a really fast car.

I am grateful the doctors removed my tumor three days ahead of my originally scheduled surgery.

I am grateful that when I heard the word "cancer," and the room started spinning, Todd was with me.

I am grateful I have an oncologist and nurses who have made my experience with chemo as good as an experience like this can possibly be.

I am grateful for an incredible family who has borne my burden and rallied in support and love for me.

I am grateful for a church family who has daily upheld me in prayer.

I am grateful for my Mary Kay network of friends and business partners who have kept my business on track in my absence, and have sustained us with food!

I am grateful for a husband who sees my new "streamlined" figure and physical changes, and still loves me with his whole being...and that in his eyes I am still beautiful.

I am grateful for children who have not stopped loving their mom.

I am grateful to be in the care of the Master Physician whose case load isn't too full for mine.

I am grateful for whatever lessons God is teaching me through this ordeal. I believe He allows trials into our lives for two purposes: (1) My good, and (2) His glory. If I live through this and come out the other end the same person as when I started–then what would the point be? If I live through this and God is not glorified or expressed through my life, then I have failed my test.

And ultimately, I am grateful to be held in the arms of a Heavenly Father Who has promised never to leave me or forsake me.

For all this, I am thankful.

LJM
November, 2002

After chemotherapy round three, my sister Gayle, who is a nurse, came from Oregon to help take care of me. She was so sweet and responsive to my needs. As much as I could, I tried to

,ıt. My mom was still helping out as well, and it did both ,ts good to have Gayle with us.

,ne time of my fourth round of chemotherapy, I had lost significant weight and was starting to feel the effects of the chemo – not just on my body, but in my mind. I realized I was only half-way through, and I was so very exhausted and riddled with side effects. I was scared, and for the first time, I considered telling Dr. Hanse that I couldn't go on. My friend Mindy took me in for a blood draw, and she encouraged me to tell Dr. Hanse how I was feeling. That was so hard for me. I was raised in a family where we finished whatever we started. Quitting wasn't an option. To voice reluctance to continue the treatments made me feel like a quitter. I told Mindy that if God set up the appointment, I would speak up. Right after my blood draw Dr. Hanse "happened" to be walking by my room. He saw me and came in. I recognized the divine appointment.

"Lori, how are you doing today?" he kindly asked.

I burst into tears. He was taken aback. I expressed how hard the chemo had been on my body, and the feelings I was having about continuing. I asked if possibly we were doing more harm than good at this point.

He listened to me with his big, compassionate eyes, and then he said, "Lori, I am so sorry you have had such a hard time of it! You should have told us sooner. This is not supposed to be so difficult, and we may have been able to ward off some of those terrible side effects with some medication. I'll make you a deal. I'll look through your charts and your test results, and when you come in for chemo on Friday, we'll talk. Maybe we can change things around and redirect our course of action. How does that sound?"

I was relieved. He had heard me. He was maybe going to change things or not make me go through the recommended three more rounds of chemo! For the first time in a long time, I felt hope. And I began to feel like this long nightmare would soon be over!

If only life were so simple ...

# Chapter Seven

Todd and I were up bright and early that Friday morning, and we went to Lafayette for my fourth chemo treatment. Or maybe not...I was anxious to hear what the doctor had to say, and, since I had found my voice, I was ready to defend my position.

We were ushered back to Dr. Hanse's office after the nurse accessed my port and drew blood. Dr. Hanse checked me over, as always, and then he sat down and rolled his chair up close to mine, which was customary for him to do when he had something important to say. The next words out of his mouth blew me away!

"Lori, what would you say if I told you today you will have your final chemo treatment? Furthermore, we are going to lessen the dosage by one-fourth, so you won't have such a hard time with the side effects."

"Don't joke around with me," I responded flatly.

"Not a joke, Lori. I wouldn't do that to you. I have reviewed your charts and your blood work, and I believe we are safe in doing only motherapy treatment and skipping the last two. The ...tments are traditionally the ones that take care of the ... is left after surgery, and the rest are the back-up ones, just ... sure we got it all. Plain and simple, I feel confident that we have eradicated your cancer."

"Then why do I need a treatment today?" I asked, as anyone in my shoes would have.

"Because I feel it's important to complete this round. Lori, we don't want you back here in a year because we stopped one cell short of getting it all."

I looked at Todd. He just gave me the look that said, "This is your decision." I thought about it, asked a few more questions, and accepted the "deal." Whew! It was hard to wrap my mind around the fact that this was going to be my last chemo treatment! We entered my little cubicle and my nurse came in smiling to begin the fourth and final treatment. It went without incident. That is, until we got home.

I began to vomit and couldn't stop. Todd called the doctor's office and they said he should bring me in as soon as possible. The car ride was awful! By the time we got to the office, all that was coming up was stomach bile. My mouth was burning and still my stomach was churning.

I was severely dehydrated. The nurses hooked up an IV and filled me with saline fluids. They discussed hospitalizing me, but once I was stabilized Dr. Hanse said it would be okay to take me home. I was relieved. I just wanted to put on my pajamas and crawl into my own bed.

Todd got me home and comfortably settled into bed, and I slept for awhile. We thought the worst was behind us. But I awakened to that horrible muscle tension in my neck and shoulders again! Oral Valium© did not take away the pain. An hour went by. My shoulders and back screamed out in pain. This was one of the worst of all the side effects. Finally, Todd called the doctor, and we found ourselves once again heading to the emergency room. After many hours, they finally got the pain under control with large doses of intravenous Valium®. I was released to go home again.

It was a relief to know that this was the last time I would have these terrible side effects. I continued to console myself with that fact, as I once again struggled to keep down food and pass the time until I was well enough to get out of bed. December had crept up on us. Christmas was coming. And so was our baby girl from China!

# Chapter Eight

When Todd and I were first married and talked about having a family, we discussed adoption. We both had a heart for orphans around the world, and decided that probably at some point we would claim one as our own.

Nate and Courtney were born and life went on. Every few years, we would revisit the adoption issue, and I would do some research. Sometimes we were discouraged because the waiting lists were so long – it might take as long as 10-15 years to adopt a Caucasian newborn through a domestic agency. Sometimes we would get discouraged because the agencies wouldn't accept us – we were able to have biological children, and already had two. Sometimes we were discouraged by the cost. We continued to discuss it now and again, knowing our hearts were open to the idea, but not feeling comfortable with the timing, agency, or cost.

That all changed in December of 1999. I was reading an article about the fate of baby girls born in China. I read how a mother usually abandoned her baby girl somewhere where she knew the baby would be found. Then the child would be placed in an overcrowded orphanage, and, if she were lucky, she would eventually be adopted. If not, she would grow up in the orphanage, where there are three workers to every 100 babies.

My heart was pulled as I read of the fate of these helpless infants who needed homes, and as I thought about the parents who were forced to abandon their baby girls because of their oppressive government. I finished the article and then asked Todd to read it. After he did, I brought up the subject of adoption again.

"Do you still want to adopt a child?"

"I have been waiting for you to be ready," he answered. "I have been ready all along."

"I'm all in!" I said. "Let's get going on this, or Nate and Courtney will be so old we'll have two separate families!"

I began research in earnest to find an adoption agency that would accept us and help us get our yearned-for child. The deeper I got into the process, the more God impressed on my heart that this was the time for us. I began to get excited.

One night in early January, we sat down with Nate and Courtney and told them that our family was going to expand through adoption. They were beyond excited, and it was great to have them on board!

Within the month, we had found an agency that accepted us; we had determined that we would adopt from China; we knew that it would most likely be a girl; we knew she would be under a year old when we got her; and, we knew we would have her in 1½ to 2 years. God opened door after door. We were convinced that He was giving us the desire of our hearts.

The paperwork took eight months to complete. At long last, in September of 2000, we were able to send our completed dossier to our agency, and within two weeks it was in China. We were told by our adoption agency that our baby should be available in December of 2002.

In October of 2002, a person from the adoption agency called us with our baby match. I'll never forget that day. We were sitting in the living room with my dear friend Ericka, and she was taking pictures as I modeled hats to see if I could give my bald, sore head a break from the wig. Soon Courtney and Nate were involved, and then even Todd was putting on hats and getting into the spirit of things. The phone rang, and after Todd answered he motioned for me to get on the other line. I stood in the doorway to the kitchen with a dorky combination of a scarf and hat on my head as I listened to the woman describe our baby girl.

She was a healthy, chubby, 7½-month-old who had been abandoned as an infant on the steps of an elementary school. Two men found her and took her to an orphanage. Her picture, along with the necessary forms, would be arriving by express mail within two days. We would need to complete the paperwork – check the box that said "Yes, we accept this child," have the paper notarized, and return it as soon as possible. If everything went as planned, we would be invited to China in December to complete the adoption and bring her home.

I just stood there and cried as Todd asked a few great questions and Ericka continued to snap pictures. Courtney was crying and dancing around. Nate was asking tons of questions. We were all so amazed and excited and thrilled. She was real. She had a name.

In two days she would have a face. This baby, whom we had carried in our hearts for almost two years now, was finally becoming more than just a stack of paperwork! God's timing is impeccable, and He knew exactly what our weary hearts needed. He even provided a photographer to capture the moment we got the news!

We went to bed that night with praise on our lips and songs in our hearts! Two days later, we received her picture. She had a beautiful round face and a crop of black hair. She was the picture of health!

When I was first diagnosed with cancer, the doctors had discouraged us from continuing with our plans to adopt. My future was so unsure, and they didn't want to see Todd's life complicated by losing me and having three children to raise alone. But immediately after Dr. Sharpe first told us I had cancer and left the room, I asked Todd, "But what about Jenna? Do you still want to go through with the adoption?"

He readily answered, "Yes! We need that baby...maybe now more than ever. How about you? Are you still in?"

"Of course! That baby needs us!" was my response. We were no more inclined to stop the adoption than we would have aborted a baby in my womb. There was no turning back.

Two weeks before Christmas, and here we were. Todd was finishing up the needed paperwork and packing. As soon as the call came, which could be any day, he would be leaving. We had already decided that I could not go. My immune system was far too compromised to go to a Third World country, and I was far too frail. I would have been a huge burden to take along. After much deliberation, we decided to ask Todd's youngest sister, Lanell, to go with him. She jumped at the opportunity.

The call came, the airline tickets were purchased, and the date was set. Todd and Lanell would be leaving December 18th. It was bittersweet. This was my baby too, and I wanted so badly to go. But, even though I would have to stay behind, we were all glad the day had finally arrived and we would very soon have our long-awaited child!

I was still fighting numerous side effects and in need of care, so Nate, Courtney, and I stayed with my parents during the kids' two-week Christmas break. My brother Kevin decided to come home from Mexico to see me and be with family. Gayle and her husband Rob also came from Oregon. It was good for me to be around the activity and the festivities. Although I missed Todd, our holiday time with my family was the balm my soul needed after four long months of battling cancer.

I was getting stronger every day, but I had setbacks, and I was concerned that I would be unable to care for our baby when we got her home. I was assured that many friends and family members were available to help. Things were going to be fine. I just needed to relax and rebuild my body.

I held baby Jenna for the first time on January 8th, 2003. She was even more beautiful than her picture, and much more therapeutic than any drug or herb! My heart soared with hope for a bright future and I looked back on my journey with a desire to glean everything God had for me to learn. We celebrated a late Christmas with our extended families. It was a very emotional time as we stopped to recognize all God had done for us the past several months. Our cups indeed ran over!

The following weeks were spent getting to know our newest family member. I gained strength daily and we were overwhelmed at the goodness of our network of friends, community, and family. Even when I had the strength to do so, there was no need for me to cook. We were constantly surrounded by friends and family bringing us food and eagerly getting to know our new baby.

A few weeks after his return from China, Todd sat down to catch up on our bookkeeping. We weren't sure where we were financially, but we were concerned. We had saved money for the adoption but had to use some of it for medical bills. Although we had received money from several churches, as well as family, friends, neighbors, and even strangers, we thought that we were deeply in debt. Somehow, and we still can't explain it, when Todd went into his office that day, he discovered that our "bill slate" was wiped clean. It was indeed a miracle from God. We wept in awe and joy.

One week later, I went to Dr. Hanse for a checkup and he reminded me of the matter we had put on hold several months previously: the unlikely possibility that I had colon cancer. I was now in remission, and he felt I was strong enough to have a colonoscopy and put our minds to rest. He scheduled it for two days later.

Before the colonoscopy, Dr. Jones reviewed with Todd and me what he was going to do. He concurred with Dr. Hanse that this was just a routine check, and they both anticipated I would come through it with flying colors. The procedure took 30 minutes, and then I found myself with Todd in a little recovery room. I was groggy, but coming around, and they were feeding me crackers and Sprite©.

Dr. Jones came in with some slides in his hand, and sat down and asked us, point blank, “Do you have a strong faith and a good support network in your family and friends?”

We assured him that we did.

“Good,” he replied, “You are going to need them. Lori, you have stage 4 colon cancer.”

# Chapter Nine

One would think that having heard the words "you have cancer" previously would have prepared me for hearing them again. It didn't. I looked at Todd. There were tears running unchecked down his face as he intently listening to Dr. Jones explain something or other.

I had a hard time focusing, and it was only partially due to the anesthetic that was still in my bloodstream. This was totally surreal. I hoped it was a dream and that I would soon wake up and go back to my new "normal" life – I was in remission, I had a new baby from China, and I was gaining strength and re-entering the world, one day at a time. Dr Jones was still talking. I strained to concentrate on what he was saying.

He was recommending surgery to remove the offending nickel-sized tumor, as well as an additional 18 inches of my colon. He felt strongly that I should have chemotherapy but he would leave that decision up to the oncologist, Dr. Hanse. With great sympathy he told us how sorry he was to be the bearer of such bad news. He would give us time to digest what we had just heard, but we needed to be in touch with his office as soon as possible to schedule surgery. He left us to our thoughts, and our tears.

I was numb. Once again I felt like my entire world was spinning out of control. And, once again, there was absolutely nothing I could do to stop it, or even slow it down. When I thought back to that time in my life, this was my assessment:

> I had just finished climbing Mt. Everest. Although I had made it to the peak, I was too weak and exhausted to even lift my head and enjoy the view. There I lay, devoid of strength, my once full backpack now empty. I was simply trying to work up enough "oomph" to begin my descent down the mountain. Forget walking, hiking, or sliding! If I could just roll. But I had no energy to do even that. When, at long last, I was able to lift my head for a peek at the view, what I saw was not the majestic wonder of an incredible panorama, but, instead, another mountain–even larger and steeper, blocking my view in all directions. Rolling down was no longer an option. My only choice was to somehow scale another incredibly high mountain! And I was to climb it with no supplies in my backpack, no strength in my body, no energy in my will. I was very much at the end of myself.
>
> It is there that God met me and said, "Lori, you need only Me. My strength is made perfect in your weakness.[ii] I have promised to never leave you or forsake you.[iii] I am here now and will continue to be with you. As you go through the valley of the shadow of death, remember that, and fear no evil. My rod and My staff will comfort you."[iv] I knew Who to cling to; I just didn't know how to find the strength to cling!

LJM

Even Todd didn't know what to say. We just sat there in shock and cried and held each other. When I regained my sense of balance, I got dressed, and Todd helped me to the car. We knew that our family and friends were anxiously awaiting our call to give them the good news. But we had no good news. We didn't even want to make the first call. We had been here before...one call leads to another, and another, and soon your strength is zapped from saying the same thing over and over, and crying with those who cry on the other end of the line. For this moment in time, we craved the comfort of silence. So we said nothing and we called no one. We just sat there, each in our own worlds, silently praying from the depths of our souls, "God, give us whatever we need to go on."

All too soon, the phone rang and broke our reverie. I listened and wept as I heard Todd explaining to my mother what we knew. We went home and had to tell the kids. Courtney crumbled. Nate left the room. Emotionally and physically exhausted, we all went to bed.

Two weeks later, I was scheduled to sing in church. I shared this testimony:

> As you probably all know, two weeks ago I was diagnosed with colon cancer. There were three things that had made the medical community certain that it wouldn't happen.
>
> First, I have no history of colon cancer anywhere in my family. Second, I am only 34 years old. Third, I have had and still have no symptoms of this disease. The doctors were left scratching their heads. Todd and I came home to adjust to the devastating news that, once again, I have to battle cancer.

On my way to church, I was thinking about what I would say to the people who asked how I was doing. Again, I found myself profoundly struck by the goodness of God. He has blessed me so abundantly. From the godly caring parents and family He placed me with at birth, to the loving, supportive stand-by-me man He gave me to marry. I have an incredible network of friends and extended family, three beautiful children who give me daily purpose, a terrific church family, and a business circle of hundreds of women to whom God has allowed me to minister. I truly am blessed!

So ponder this. My daughter asked me, "Why does God keep allowing bad things to happen to us? Haven't we been through enough already?" Good question. Very good question. I think it's on more than a few minds these days. My answer to her was, I believe, an answer for her heart directly from God. And that is this...

In the banquet of life, God determines what we will be served. It's usually some meat, potatoes, vegetables, and dessert. I realized that I have been eating cheesecake for 34 years.

He has over and over again blessed me with goodness from His hand. Just in these past few months, He has chosen to serve me spinach. I don't like the taste of it, and I don't really want to eat it, but as Job said many years ago, "Who am I to accept the good from God and not the bad?" You see, the same God who is holding the spoonfuls of my blessings is serving me spinach. And I have every confidence in the One who holds the spoon.

I, of course, dread the surgery, the recovery time, and the uncertainties of my future. I hate the fact that my family and friends have to go through this with me again. But ultimately, if you were to ask me how I am doing, I would respond to you, from the very depths of my heart, "It is well with my soul."

LJM
February, 2003

My sister Debbie and her fiancé Mark had planned their wedding for mid-February. I so wanted to be there. I could not have been happier for them, and it was like healing balm to my soul to witness something good happening in our family. We discussed the wedding with Dr. Jones, who said we could postpone the surgery for ten days so I could go. Dr. Hanse had reviewed the results of the colon-oscopy and he concurred. Debbie was a radiant bride, and I was able to stand by her side as they exchanged vows.

The day after the wedding, I began to drink a gallon of salt water stuff, again prepping for surgery. The next day I was at the hospital for yet another major surgery. After being admitted, I changed into the beautiful hospital gown, and then asked the nurse when I could get my cap. (I remembered that they had put a little blue cap on my head before my previous surgeries.) The look on her face made me think she had never before had a patient who was anxious to wear that blue thing. But I was. I had a very bald head, which I did not want anyone to see, under my wig. When she brought it to me, she said, "You don't have to put this on. We will do that for you when you get back to the operating room." She left the room. I shed the wig and put on the cap.

As before, the anesthesiologist came into the cubicle and explained to Todd and me what he was going to do. Dr. Jones came in as well, and this time he was the one to initiate prayer. Then they both left to go scrub, and Todd and I held each other silently.

I can't imagine what it was like for him to see me, once again, going in for major cancer surgery. I know he was scared, but he put on such a brave front for me. I was trying to do the same for him. In the meantime, the waiting room was filling with family and friends with whom he would spend the next four hours – praying, talking, encouraging one another. One common thread, their love for me, had brought each of them to this hospital waiting room at this point in time.

When the nurse came back to wheel me away, and I had to let go of Todd's hand, I felt very alone. But at that very moment I sensed the very real presence of my Heavenly Father right there on that gurney with me. As I was wheeled into the operating room once again, I heard Him whisper softly, "I told you I will never leave you. I am here with you now."[v] I felt comforted, and I was able to acknowledge that not only was He "walking through the valley"[vi] with me, but He had prepared that valley, if you will, beforehand. Every person in that room, from Dr. Jones to the nurses to the attendants to the anesthesiologist, He had gathered together, putting the players in place and preparing the way. He was very much in control. My fate lay not in the hands of those doctors, but in the much more capable hands of the Master Physician. As I began to count backwards from 100, I was at peace in my heart.

# Chapter Ten

In every respect, my experiences with cancer were so out-of-the-ordinary; there was no case quite like mine in the textbooks. For some reason, it did my heart good to be an anomaly. It was comforting to know that this wasn't going to happen to those I loved just because it happened to me.

When I awakened from surgery this time, it was with a relief that was so sweet! I had pain, sure, but this time it was nothing like after the hysterectomy surgery! I didn't realize how very afraid I was of waking up...until I was actually awake and realized the pain was bearable. During the next eight days in the hospital, I healed well and the surgeon was pleased with my progress.

I had a lot of time to think while I was in the hospital. I also had a lot of time to pray. I had such an incredible, inexplicable fear of chemotherapy. I kept praying that my oncologist would say the surgery took care of the cancer and I would not have to go through chemo again. I pled, "Lord, please, no more chemo!"

Once I was home from the hospital, neighbors, friends, and family once again rallied to support us. The outpouring of their gifts, encouragement, notes, babysitting, financial help, house cleaning, and so much more was a blessing from God.

I found it very hard to not be able to lift or care for our precious little Jenna. One day, when I was alone with her for a short time, she woke up and was very unhappy! My "mommy's heart" couldn't bear to let her lie in the next room and cry. So, clutching a pillow tightly to my incision, I slowly got out of bed and made my way to her room. I leaned over her crib and tried to comfort her, but she kept getting more and more agitated. She was right there, but I couldn't lift her out and care for her, and she couldn't get to me! I was extremely frustrated, and finally came up with a plan.

I retrieved a little stool from the next room, set it beside Jenna's crib, and very carefully stepped up onto it. The sides of the crib were down, so I could climb over the side. As soon as I was in the crib lying down beside her, Jenna quieted. Although she seemed a bit perplexed, she knew that I was there for her, and that was good enough!

I had already been told that I had the most advanced, stage 4 colon cancer. Now it was time for my follow-up appointment with Dr. Hanse. Again and again I prayed that he would not tell me I had to have chemotherapy again.

Todd and I were greeted by the nurses and staff at Dr. Hanse's office. In some ways it felt comfortable to be surrounded by the familiar. But in other ways, I couldn't believe that I was here again, within six weeks of being in remission from the ovarian cancer.

While Todd and I waited for the doctor, I said, "I won't do chemo. I can't. It almost killed me the first time, and I won't put my body through it again. I love you and the kids, and I am willing to fight to live, but my fight plan cannot include chemo. I am firm on this. Please back me up."

What could he say? He knew what I said was true. There I sat, a bald, 100-pound shell of my former self. There was no denying the incredible toll that chemo and its side effects had taken. But he loved me; he didn't want to let the disease take me away from him and the kids. If chemo was the only way to keep me alive, then he was going to support chemo. He said as much, and then added, "Let's see what Dr. Hanse says. Don't rule anything out yet."

Dr. Hanse came in. He had a somber look on his face, and he spoke once again with great sympathy. He reviewed with us the implications of having stage 4 cancer. "Lori, I know you hate it, and I am so sorry, but I have to recommend chemotherapy. We have no way of knowing if the chemo for your ovarian cancer killed the colon cancer cells in your body. We can't just sit back and hope so. We have to take aggressive action, and it needs to be soon."

I began to weep. Dr. Hanse looked at me and said, "You know what I think we need to do, but you have to be physically and emotionally able to face chemo. I strongly suggest that you get a second opinion. Let me give you some names of other oncologists."

Todd and I assured Dr. Hanse that we had great confidence in him, and didn't want to go to another doctor. Although he was flattered, he did not waver in his response. Regardless of what we decided, he would remain my primary physician but he felt it imperative that we get another opinion. He would do whatever it took to get me well again; my health was the first and foremost issue.

We left there with a follow-up appointment, and the names of three oncologists.

# Chapter Eleven

When I was first diagnosed with cancer, we were inundated with information about various approaches to treatment. People who deeply cared about me were swamping us with articles from newspapers, magazines, and medical journals. But I was too weak to look at, let alone assess, the tons of information. I just passed everything on to my mom who read all that she could and, in addition, did online research.

The first cancer and subsequent treatment happened so quickly that we followed the doctors' recommendations without exploring other options. By the second time around, however, we all had many questions about the best course of action. Todd and my parents had watched as first the cancer, next the surgeries, and finally the chemo were draining the life from me. We all knew how frail I was and even though conventional treatment called for more chemo, without something to build up my body as we went along, the chemo itself would take my life.

Although I am far from being a "health nut," Todd and I began to research non-traditional treatment options. We were drawn to the programs that offered nutritional support for the body along with conventional medicine. My mother's labor of love – hours and hours of research time – resulted in the choice of three facilities for us to consider. The first was in California; if I went there for treatment, I would need to stay for as long as three months at a time. I immediately ruled that out. This was my second cancer in five short months; I had already spent too much time away from those I loved. If I was going to die soon, I wanted to be with my family as much as possible before then.

Option number two was a doctor in Chicago, known for non-conventional chemotherapy combined with a nutritional plan to build up the patient's body even as the chemo destroyed healthy cells. Todd vetoed this one because we did not have insurance coverage for this sort of treatment.

We chose option number three: Cancer Treatment Centers of America (CTCA). One of their five facilities is north of Chicago – about 3½ hours drive from our home. This hospital accepted our insurance, and offered exactly what we were looking for: a scientific approach to fighting cancer, along with a nutritional program to build the body. The staff included nutritionists, naturopathic doctors, physical therapists, oncologists, clergy, technicians, psychiatrists, massage therapists, and acupuncturists. It was a go! We scheduled an appointment for the first of March. They told us to come prepared for three days of testing, and to pack for a hospital stay, in case I chose to be admitted at the end of that time.

Courtney had a particularly hard time with the idea of my leaving again. When I told her that I might be gone for a week, she cried and cried. She had been without her mom quite enough; this was simply too much. Even though it wrenched my heart to leave her, I knew I had to proceed.

We found the CTCA hospital in a quaint little Illinois town called Zion, where every street is named after a Biblical character or place. The hospital itself was much smaller than the one where I had my surgeries, and it had a calm, quiet feel. Todd and I went to the 3rd floor where we filled out a ream of paperwork, and then sat down in the spacious waiting room. As we looked around the room, we saw people of many nationalities. There were bald women and men. There were people in wheelchairs, and people who looked as healthy as Todd. There were those with cancer as young as I, and still others who were even younger.

Cancer is no respecter of persons. It is not reserved for the aged or the malnourished or for those with cancer in their family history. It strikes whomever, whenever, and wherever it pleases. This became painfully obvious as we observed and got to know many of the patients at CTCA.

Some patients, like me, were at CTCA for the first time. Many were there for their two, five, or even twenty-year checkups, having been in remission that long. I met survivors of leukemia as well as lung, pancreatic, breast, prostate, liver, ovarian, uterine, bone, and colon cancer. There was an air of hope as the stories of survivors were inter-mixed with the stories of us "newcomers." Although I was scared, I felt at peace. This was where we were supposed to be.

The next three days were a whirlwind of activity. I saw more specialists and teams of doctors, and went through more tests than I can recall. What I do remember, however, is meeting many wonderful people as we were ushered in and out of that big waiting room.

The experience that undoubtedly had the greatest impact on me occurred the second day we were there. Todd and I were sitting in a small waiting room, and I was drinking the nasty tasting barium in preparation for a CT scan. There were two people sitting across from us. I would have been chatting, which is my nature, but it was too hard to talk and concentrate on getting the barium to stay down at the same time. I kept peering at them over my cup as I slowly downed the gunk. The man had gray hair and was significantly older than the woman. She appeared to be in her late 20's–petite, with sparkly blue eyes and a cute pixy hair-do. Were they married? Were they brother and sister? Which one was the patient? (It was safe to assume that someone had cancer; after all, this was a cancer hospital.) I took another swig, made a face, and complained yet again to Todd about the nasty stuff, when, unexpectedly, the woman leaned over to me and put her hand on my knee. "I'm sorry to tell you this," she said with a distinct Wisconsin accent. "But when you finish that cupful of barium, they are going to bring you another one!"

They introduced themselves: Rick and Jodi Lind, husband and wife from Eau Claire, Wisconsin. He was 12 years her senior, and they had three kids, Kaitlyn, who was 8; Nate, who was 4; and Ciera, who was 2. And Jodi was the one with cancer. They, too, had come to CTCA to explore the possibility of an alternative to chemotherapy. Jodi had been diagnosed with breast cancer a year before, had tried chemotherapy and almost died from the side effects, and then had tried a strict regimen of nutrition. But her tumor was continuing to grow, so they were looking for another treatment alternative. They had arrived the day before we had, so they were on their last day of testing. They "happened" to be in that waiting room because one of her test results was not clear, and she had to have another brain scan. Later in the day they would be meeting with the oncologist.

To my dismay, I was called in to have my CT scan before I was able to get to know Jodi better. She drew me like a moth to a flame. In just a short time I learned that she was about my age, and had three children at home like I did. I also learned that Jodi and I shared a faith in the same powerful God. We vowed to try to get together in the big waiting room later.

My CT scan was awful. The technician refused to use my port, so he had to access one of my veins, which was somewhat collapsed as a result of the chemo. I begged for Todd to be allowed to be with me to hold my hand while they accessed my vein. My request was refused. I begged the tech to use my port, telling him I would take full responsibility if something went wrong. This request was also refused. The tech was very curt, and it occurred to me that either he was a very cold person or he was having a very bad day.

By the time my test was done, I was traumatized sufficiently to have forgotten all about Jodi. But when we got back into the main waiting room, Rick and Jodi were waiting for us. They had met with the oncologist and decided to follow his recommendation: Jodi would check into the hospital the next morning to begin treatment. She was bubbling with excitement! She was anxious to get started with her treatment so she could get back home to her family.

Somewhere in the middle of much conversation, she asked me, "Lori, if you decide to check in here, too, can we be roomies?" I responded that I would love that, but we were unsure whether or not I was staying. I briefly explained what I had just gone through in the

CT room, and she smiled that engaging smile. She told me that she, too, had a bad experience there, but she would save her story for later. Then they left for their hotel. We made plans to touch base the next day.

After they left, Todd and I sat in a corner of the waiting room discussing the pros and cons of my being treated at this facility. The whole hospital had the air of hope and healing, there were helpful nurses and attendants, with one exception – the CT technician. It was as if he didn't get the memo that said, "Be nice to the patients." We knew that if I stayed, I would again be in his care. My experience with the CT tech was almost enough for us to decide not to stay at CTCA.

At that point we put our decision on hold. We had one more appointment for the day, a meeting with the nutritionist. We were also scheduled to meet with the oncologist the next morning. He would brief us on my test results, and make a recommendation for my treatment.

The nutritionist, Jamie, was young with dark hair and kind eyes. She took a complete history of my dietary habits, and we talked at length about how I could improve my health from a nutritional standpoint. She delved into my former eating disorder of anorexia from my teenage and early adult years. She outlined a few days' worth of meals and snacks, and suggested other foods to begin rebuilding my frail body.

Todd and I asked questions of Jamie that went far beyond healthy eating, including ones about the facility itself. We later learned that we were her last appointment for the day, and, in spite of a 1½ hour commute through Chicago traffic, she stayed an hour past our scheduled time to answer our many questions.

But Jamie gave us even more than her expertise and time. She had sensed a reserve in us from the moment that she walked in the room. After she had done her job as a nutritionist, she gently asked what else was bothering me. I broke down and wept, as I shared with her the rough treatment I had received from the technician. She excused herself from the room for a moment. When she returned, she told us that, without using my name, she had reported the incident to the person in charge of the CT scans. She then brought in the hospital's head nurse who apologized profusely for how I had been treated. They both reiterated that the treatment I had received was not what this hospital was about, and assured me that the incident would be brought to the attention of the proper authorities. The head nurse left, but Jamie stayed with us until she was sure we were okay.

The kindness and sincerity of this young woman helped us to make our decision about treatment. She is the reason we decided to come back the next day to meet with Dr. Morgan. We thank God for her!

# Chapter Twelve

The next morning, we checked out of the hotel and made our way to the hospital. As we entered the CTCA, we observed someone being brought into the emergency room; Todd grabbed and squeezed my hand as our thoughts went back to the many times I was the one being hurried through the hospital doors. I was weak and frail, for sure, but I was standing, and still alive by God's grace. He had brought us through so much.

Dr. Morgan was a man of small-stature and Middle Eastern descent. He was soft-spoken but possessed an air of authority and knowledge. He gave me a thorough check-up, and then began to explain how this hospital worked.

"Everything I'm telling you today has been reviewed by a team of oncologists. We met yesterday. Included in our group were an ovarian cancer specialist, and two colon cancer specialists. We went over all of your scans, reports, tests, and surgery results from back home, as well as the tests that you had done here these past few days." He paused and looked straight at me, "I understand you had a difficult time with your CT. I am sorry about that. You deserve to be treated better."

Dr. Morgan continued. "After our meeting and further study on my part, this is our conclusion. We believe that the colon cancer was there before the ovarian cancer. Colon cancer inside the colon usually doesn't grow very aggressively. The tumor you had removed could well have been there a year or more before they found it. Fortunately, before it got out of hand, your ovarian tumor developed and, through that, they found the colon cancer. In an odd turn of events, the ovarian cancer may well have saved your life. At any rate, because the colon cancer has been there so long, and quite possibly was the cause of the ovarian tumor, we recommend chemotherapy specifically designed to target and kill colon cancer cells. Although the surgery could have gotten all the colon cancer, we can't be sure. We aren't comfortable letting you go without treatment, and chemotherapy is the only way to be sure we have killed all the floating cells."

I started that dazed, this-can't-be-happening-again, feeling. My ears were pounding with ocean-wave sounds, and I felt faint. Todd and Dr. Morgan both noticed, and the doctor buzzed his nurse to bring me a Sprite© to get my blood sugar levels up. When I was stabilized, he continued. "We are recommending six complete rounds of chemo, followed by quarterly check-ups and CT scans for five years. First-time patients are usually checked into the hospital for the first round of chemo, so that they can be kept under 24-hour surveillance for the duration of the treatment. Unlike most cancer treatment clinics, we will give you the same prescribed dosage as your home oncologist recommended, but we will spread it over a five-day period. We believe that by doing it slowly and at lower doses, your body has more time to adjust to it and, hopefully, avoid unwanted side effects. I understand that you had a very hard time when you underwent chemo?"

I nodded. Todd described a few of the many side effects that I had experienced.

Dr. Morgan went on to explain that the nutrition program as well as the recommendations of the naturopath would play a huge role in helping lessen side effects.

I had one question: "Am I going to lose my hair again?" Although my hair was naturally blonde and straight, it had grown back curly and black. I liked the feeling of having hair, and I wasn't too eager to lose it again.

Dr. Morgan nodded and I went numb. My whole being seemed to be screaming, "I can't go through all of this again!" I had come for a second opinion hoping I would find someone who wouldn't recommend chemo!

Todd was, again, asking some very good questions, and the doctor was answering them as well as he could. They seemed to be stuck on one particular question: "How did this happen? Was the ovarian cancer caused by the colon cancer, the colon cancer caused by the ovarian cancer, or were they entirely separate?" Dr. Morgan admitted that he and his team of experts were still stymied. Far from a textbook case, I had stumped the doctors. They had no answers.

He said he'd give us time alone to think about all he had said, and we should call him if we had any more questions. We could stay in the room as long as we needed, and then let his nurse know what we decided. We thanked him, and he excused himself and left.

The CTCA is located by a beautiful pond. I walked over to the window and gazed at ducks swimming around so peacefully and naturally. They made life look so easy and normal. My life, by stark contrast, had just gotten even more complicated than it had already been. I started to cry. Todd put his arms around me and we stood there in silence for a few minutes.

"I know what you are thinking, Sweetie," he finally said, "But we need to make a decision today. Are we both going home tonight and coming back in a week or so for your treatment? Or, am I leaving you here, and coming back for you in a week? Or, are we going to ignore all the doctors and walk out right now? End of the road. No more tests, no more chemo, just quit. You know how I feel, but, Lori, this is your body, and it is ultimately your decision. I will support whatever you decide."

"I want to fight this. I want to know that I have done all I can, and that even if I die, you and the kids will know I gave it my all. But, chemo again – I just don't know if I can take it!" I was still in tears.

"Lori, I know you. You are a fighter. You always finish what you start. I believe you will be able to handle it this time because of all of the support this place offers. If we check you in, and they start the chemo, and you get awful side effects, you just say 'stop!' and I will come and get you. It can be over if you want it to be. I want you to know you have a choice."

I had been struggling with the issue of choice for some time. Everywhere I went – from my first surgery, to the chemo, to the second surgery, to this – I felt like those in the medical community were telling me what to do with my body. I felt like I wasn't in charge, like I had no say in the matter. Knowing that Todd was sensitive to my feelings by making it clear that I did have a choice somewhat calmed my nerves. "If we are going to do this, then just leave me here. I want to get started so I can get it over with. Call the nurse and let's do this thing!" I responded flatly.

"Are you sure?"

"Yes. Let's get it done."

With that, Todd gave me another gentle squeeze and called in the nurse. We went through another whole ream of paperwork and met the nurse who would be our case manager. She took us to the second floor where I was to be admitted, and scheduled my chemo treatments over the next five months.

The case manager then introduced us to the nurses on the 2nd floor, and one of them said they were getting my room ready. My case manager excused herself, Todd went to the car to get my overnight bag, and I sat on a chair in the hallway and took in my surroundings. Everyone was wearing white, blending right into the colorless walls. The place was totally sterile and smelled of disinfectant. So, this was to be my life for the next five months: coming here for a week at a time, getting back into the whole yucky chemo thing, and then hoping and praying that it worked. The CTCA was an interesting place to visit, but I didn't want to stay here. It took all of my resolve not to bolt.

Todd returned as they were showing me my room. I requested rooming with Jodi, and they were looking into it. Todd and I had a tearful good-bye. He was as unsettled as I, but we both were hopeful that chemo would be more tolerable at this hospital. We prayed together, and he left with a promise to bring the kids up to see me in two days. And then I was alone.

Sitting on the edge of the bed, I looked around my drab room. "God, are You here? I am feeling scared and alone. I don't want to be here. Please be here with me. Show me that this is the right decision. I need You."

"Go find Jodi." The words were as clear as if they'd been spoken out loud. No doubt that God was nudging me. I cleaned the tear streaks off my cheeks and reapplied my lipstick. Then I went to the nurse's station and asked where I could find Jodi Lind. She was in Room 24.

"Can I go in and see her?" I asked.

"Her naturopath is with her right now. But you may go in to see her in 20 minutes or so."

"Thank you."

I meandered down the hall and found her room. The door was open and I could hear voices. I took a seat in the hall and waited. In a few minutes, someone came out of the room, acknowledged me, and walked on.

I peaked into the room. Jodi was lying in her bed getting chemo. She was resting with her eyes closed. I didn't want to disturb her, so I turned to leave. She heard my shuffle.

"Lori! You came! I heard you are going to be my roomie as soon as they get the bed ready. I am so excited! How are you?"

That was the beginning of three of the most incredible days of my cancer-ridden life. I sat on her bed and we began to talk – not just about surface things, but about real, gut-level things that only people who had walked our paths could share. We expressed our fears, our hopes for the future, our belief that God is in control of all things, including our being together at that moment. We laughed, and we cried.

Meanwhile, a nurse moved my stuff to the room and pronounced me an official occupant of Room 24. I made my way over to my bed eventually, and, as it was getting late, I put on my pajamas and offered to help Jodi do the same.

Once we were both settled in, a nurse started my chemo. They would administer my first 5-hour dose while I slept. I liked that idea. Maybe I could sleep through the symptoms. Thankfully, the Benadryl® knocked me out, as usual.

I awakened mid-morning to see Jodi sitting in the chair at the end of our beds. She was dressed, with hair styled and make-up on. "Good-morning, sleepy-head," she said.

I sat up slowly. There was an ache in my body and a terrible metallic taste in my mouth, both familiar side effects of chemo. I noticed that saline, the usual, was hanging from one pole; but there were no other bags. My first round of chemo must be done.

A half-hour later, I was freshly showered and putting on my make-up, propped up in my bed. Jodi and I began to chat some more, but kept being interrupted by members of the staff – the pain relief team, the nutritionist, the physical therapists, the case workers, the naturopaths, the oncologists, the psychiatrist, and many more.

Periodically, they would close the curtain between our beds to allow for privacy, but, as soon as they would leave, we would update each other on what we were being told.

Such was the case when the psychiatrist, Dr. Benson, came in to see me. He was a small, soft-spoken man with an inviting, non-intimidating manner. He started asking questions, and I found myself wanting to talk to him. I didn't foresee it at the time, but this gentle man would end up being a critical part of my care. He might even have saved my life.

At this first meeting, we talked about the sleep problems that had haunted me for so long. He diagnosed me with restless leg syndrome and prescribed a sleep aid. That night, I slept more soundly than I had in months, and I woke up feeling refreshed.

Dr. Benson and I also delved into my history of eating disorders, a touchy subject for me. In short, I had battled anorexia nervosa since I was 14 years old. Although I had some periods when the disease didn't plague me as much, this was an on-going, unresolved issue. We talked at length and scheduled another appointment as he was determined to help me as much as possible while I was there.

When I was first diagnosed with cancer, I weighed about 123 pounds, not a lot for someone who is 5 feet 9 inches tall. I always fell short on the weight charts in the doctor's offices, but I was okay with that. Before cancer entered my body, I was healthy. But I had been controlled by anorexia at several points in my life: during a tough time in high school, when I was first married and living in a community that was foreign to me, several other times during the next 14 years, and now, while I was battling cancer.

It seemed strange to me that an eating disorder would haunt me at this particular phase in life. After all, cancer and chemotherapy combined are a very effective weight-loss method. Since my diagnosis, I had lost 23 pounds. I had managed to regain a few pounds since my last surgery, but now, with the resumption of the chemo regimen and the accompanying side effects, I was sure to lose more weight. Because Dr. Benson was very concerned about that probability, he asked permission to talk to my nutritionist so they could work together. I consented and told him about the lengthy talk I had already had with her. He felt reassured that we were all three on the same page.

Dr. Benson walked out, and Jodi and I were finally free of visitors for awhile. We shared our life stories, prayed, sang, talked about our families, listened in on each other's phone conversations, cried together, assisted each other through bouts of nausea and endless trips to the bathroom, and continued to bond at deeper and deeper levels.

I rarely recall a time in Room 24 when one of us was not sitting on the end of the other's bed. At one point, I said to Jodi,

"Jod, do you think we are being too loud? I mean, there are people down the hall who have cancer! Shouldn't we be quieter and more respectful of them?"

Jodi burst into a gurgling laugh. She looked at me, my wig hanging on a bedside post and chemo dripping into my veins. "Lori, we have cancer too! If we want to handle it this way, we are entitled!" From that point on, I decided not to concern myself with the sounds of song and laughter coming from our room.

On one occasion, we started giggling that uncontrollable, eye-watering, we-don't-even-know-why-it's-funny laughter. Just then, in walked a nurse.

I glanced at Jodi with an "I-told-you-so" look! No doubt we were in trouble now. I regained my composure enough to ask the nurse, "So, which one of us are you in here to poke?" I thought it safe to assume there was a needle somewhere on her person. Then I pointed to Jodi and quickly added, "I hope it's her!"

"Actually, I'm not in here to poke either one of you," she replied, rather gingerly. "I am on a 15-minute break, and I wondered if I could spend it in here with you. You see, out there, it is silent and tomb-like as we work with despondent cancer patients in varying stages of the disease. But I hear laughter coming from this room and echoing down the halls. I hear fun and life and joy. I will be quiet and sit over to the side and not intrude, but may I spend my break in here with you two?"

We were taken aback, but immediately accommodating. "Not only can you spend your break in here with us," Jodi answered, "But let us share with you the Source of our joy – our Friend Jesus."

That was the first of many nurses who found their way into our room during their breaks. There was something (or, more precisely Someone) that drew them to us. Here we were...two young mothers, each engaged in a grueling battle with cancer. But we allowed laughter and fun times to overrule the darkness of the disease and our circumstances.

Jodi and I were so "on the same page," and had gotten to know each other so quickly and so deeply; the nurses could hardly believe we had just met. But, three days later, when Jodi received a call from her husband, I soon realized he was coming the next day to take her home. As I listened to their conversation, I began to feel very alone. I knew that when Jodi left Room 24, so did the laughter, the caring, the singing, the friend sitting on the end of my bed. My attitude began to turn sour as I contemplated being alone.

At that moment I turned to the Source of comfort to whom I had gone since I was a little girl. I picked up my Bible from my bedside table. I leafed through it, looking for words of encouragement and strength from my Heavenly Father. I read in Joshua 1,

> *Be strong and courageous, do not be afraid or discouraged for the Lord your God is with you wherever you go.*

I thumbed through the Psalms until I came across Psalm 94:1:

> *When doubts filled my mind, your comfort gave me renewed hope and cheer. The Lord is my fortress, my mighty rock where I can hide.*

Then I read from Hebrews 12:12, 13:

> *So take a new grip with your tired hands and stand firm on your shaky legs, mark out a straight path for your feet. Then those who follow you, though they are weak and lame, will not stumble and fall, but they will become strong.*

My heart was a bit encouraged as I turned my attention back to Jodi's phone conversation. She was talking to Ciera, her 2 year old. I overheard something like this, "Really? Kaitlyn helped you do that? You need to thank your sister for being so kind. You drew a picture for me? Wow! I can't wait for you to show it to me! What about Mommy? Well, I'm having a slumber party with my new friend Lori. We are laughing and talking and eating Jell-o© and having a good time! I wish you could be here with us!"

A slumber party!? I looked around, and with my earthly eyes I saw only hospital beds, chemo poles, and the stark whiteness of the sterile room. Drab. Uninviting. Dull. Then the Holy Spirit got a grip on my heart: "Lori, observe my servant Jodi. Do as she is doing. Live like she is living. I didn't allow you to have cancer so you could merely survive until it is over and then get on with living as you knew it before. You need to learn to thrive! Live out loud! Remember, 'This is the day that the Lord has made. Rejoice and be glad in it!'"[vii]

So much for my pity party! The Lord used Jodi that day to teach me a lesson that I will always remember. Life can be a party, if you want it to be. Jodi woke up each morning and chose to have a great day, in spite of her circumstances! I must do the same.

I also remembered a quote I had often heard from Mary Kay: "Life is 10% what happens to you and 90% how you respond to it." I had been living that backwards. I was so thankful for Jodi's example – and God's Word – to get me back on track.

At that moment I knew I was going to be okay. God was still with me, and He was definitely still on the throne!

The next day played out exactly as I had imagined. Rick came from Wisconsin to get Jodi. They packed her bags and left, with a promise that we would see each other again in a few weeks.

I was alone in Room 24.

# Chapter Thirteen

A couple of days later I was back home, where my family and I once again experienced God's provision for us through people who helped bear our burdens in very practical ways. After my chemo sessions, my mother lived with us during the week, to help care for me and keep the household running smoothly. Neighbors and friends, including many from our church and my Mary Kay units, as well as people we didn't even know, provided meals. My neighbor Lois had become indispensable as she cleaned the house, brought us groceries, carpooled for the two older kids, and helped out however and wherever she was needed.

My friend and neighbor, Kelly, cared for Jenna almost daily, refusing to let us pay her. A group of ladies from her church gave us money to help defray the cost of my treatments and other expenses. We saw how very blessed we were!

Meanwhile, I wasn't handling the chemo very well. Although I was taking a different kind of medication that helped some, the side effects were taking a toll on me. For a full week after each round of chemotherapy, I was pretty much "down for the count," able to do only small chores, like fold a load of laundry or put a pre-made casserole into the oven. I longed to be an active participant in the lives of my family members, but, for the most part, I was only a bystander, observing them living their lives.

In the meantime, my Mary Kay business was in very capable hands. My dear friend and sister-in-law, Amy, who was my administrative assistant when I was diagnosed in September, kept the business running like a well-oiled machine. My directors stood in for me on meeting nights, and one of them, Ericka, along with her unit, had a fund-raiser that brought in enough money to pay for an entire week's stay at the CTCA. So many people stepped up that the business was not a concern for me. In fact, Amy distinctly told me to concentrate on getting better, and leave the business to her.

Todd and I continued to have concerns about our son Nate. He was cocooning to protect himself from the trauma associated with my two bouts with cancer, along with the surgeries and chemo. As his mother, a part of me wanted to allow him to stay in his self-spun cocoon where he was likely to be less vulnerable to the circumstances that were permeating our family life. But another part of me was frustrated with him for not acknowledging the reality of what was going on around him.

One day, Amy called. She was having a hard time coming to terms with my 2nd cancer diagnosis, and needed to talk to me about how I was doing. I decided to take the call upstairs so the kids wouldn't have to hear me talk about myself and cancer once again. When I told them I was leaving the room for a private conversation, Nate said, "What's wrong, Mom?"

I answered rather curtly, "I have a friend on the phone whose friend is battling cancer and she is really struggling. I want to talk to her in private."

"Who has cancer, Mom?" was his reply. I was stunned. I talked to Todd and others: Nate's youth leader, my dad, Nate's best friend's mother. I pleaded with them to help me get through to him. They all tried, but none succeeded.

One night, I went into Nate's room to talk to him. He was fiddling around with Legos© and I asked if we could talk a minute. He shrugged an assent.

"Nate," I began, "I just want to say how sorry I am that cancer has entered our lives. We don't want it, but it won't go away. It has had a huge effect on all of us, and I know it has totally shaken your world. You want to just be a normal kid, but because of the stigma of having a mom with cancer, you are always bombarded with questions about me and my health. I know you love me and that it has been very hard on you, and I just want to express to you that I know how you are feeling. I love you, son."

He never looked up as I was speaking. He just kept playing with his Legos©. But I noticed that they weren't turning into a masterpiece, as they usually did for him. I moved to leave the room, and he said, "Mom?"

I turned. "What, son?"

"It is really hard for me to, well, talk about things, and to, um, well, express myself. I'm just not good at that."

"I know, Nate. It's okay. I know how you feel even though you aren't able to talk about it," I responded.

He looked up, tears glistening in his eyes, and said, simply, "Thank you, Mom."

"You're welcome. Good night." I left his room hopeful that maybe there had finally been a breakthrough.

A few weeks later, Todd and I saw an advertisement for the sale of basset hound puppies. Nate had always wanted a basset hound, so we decided to buy him one. I was so pleased to be able to do something positive for him in the midst of an otherwise dreary life. He was elated! The puppy, which we named Droopy, was adorable. Watching him and our other dog, Nicki, romp around the yard was as therapeutic for me as it was fun for Nate. But only 2½ weeks after Droopy had become a part of our family, he ran onto the highway and was hit and killed. It was then that Nate broke down and cried like never before. All of his pent-up emotion was released in his expression of grief over his lost puppy. After that he was much more open about what was going on in our lives. Before one of my significant medical tests, he said to me, "Mom, I know it is so much easier to say it than to live it, but I really think that everything is going to be alright. I am praying for you."

I now understand what my son was doing inside his cocoon. He was praying. He was being stretched, and he was growing spiritually by leaps and bounds. When he finally emerged towards the end of his 7th grade year, his relationship with God was closer than it had ever been before. He was no longer a boy; he had become a young man.

Courtney was also continuing to have a rough time. We always knew where she was emotionally, because she cried whenever she felt like it and freely shared her feelings with all of us – her father, her grandmother, her friends, and me. But she was having a very difficult 5th grade year. Normally an excellent student who completed her assignments punctually, she was finding it impossible to get her homework done. Making it even more difficult, she had a teacher who expected top performance from her students, regardless of what was going on in their personal lives. Todd supported Courtney by writing notes to her teacher, and my mother helped her with her homework. (My mom was also there to console Courtney the day of my colon surgery, when her favorite kitty was run over by the school bus!)

Courtney has had a deep relationship with God ever since she accepted Jesus as her personal Savior in 2nd grade. But her faith was stretched to the max that year, as she watched me dwindle to a shell of my former self, battling two types of cancer in a row. She and I talked about it one evening. She had been in church and heard the testimonies I had shared. She knew that I was at peace inwardly and was trusting God with my life. But she asked, simply, "Mommy, how can you be okay with this? I want to be okay, but I'm not!"

"Courtney, God promises to give us the grace we need as we travel through the dark valleys." I replied. "What you are seeing is simply His grace given to me at this time. It's okay to not understand. It's okay to ask 'Why?' Our God made us human. He made us to be dependent on Him. He is big enough to handle any of our questions, or doubts, or fears. So when you are hurting or mad or sad, just talk to Him. He won't stop loving you because you are upset with the way our life is right now."

"But I want the grace that He has given you!" she sobbed. "I am struggling, too. Why don't I have the grace that you have and the perspective that it's okay because He is in charge? When we love Him so much, why is He letting all this bad stuff happen to us?"

"I wish I had the answers, sweetheart. I just know that He is in control of all aspects of our lives, and He has not forgotten us. He has not forgotten you. He has wonderful things planned for your life, and He is molding you into someone great through this huge trial. Already I see such maturity in you that I certainly didn't have at your age. It's hard, I know. You want to know that I am going to be okay. You want this to all go away. That is where we need to just trust Him." Then I gave her the spinach vs. cheesecake example – that in life's banquet, God chooses what we will be served. For me, it had been cheesecake for 34 years, but now it was spinach. Who was I to question the One who held the spoon? She thought on that long and hard.

Jenna took the whirlwind of our lives in stride! She knew only that Mommy was gone every now and then, and that during those times someone else cared for her. She will never remember those days, but I will always be grateful that she entered our lives when she did. I had questioned God's timing and the fact that I was unable to go along to China to get her. But, as always, God knew what He was doing, and He knew I would need her at this time in my life. Even during the times that I was not able to lift her or care for her, it was so therapeutic to lie on the couch and watch as she discovered her toes and fingers, or tried to roll over, or reached for the toys around her. My mother observed that Jenna brought a long-lost sparkle of hope to my eyes.

During this time, Jodi and I often talked on the phone. Shortly after our days together at CTCA, I learned that she had gotten so sick after her chemo treatment that she had to be admitted to a hospital to be treated for dehydration. Jodi would not be going back to the CTCA for chemotherapy and we prayed with her and Rick for wisdom as they explored other options.

Jodi and I stayed in touch by phone a few times a week. I found in her the "circumstantial soul-mate" I so desperately needed. She felt the same way about me. I was very disappointed I would not see her when I had my next treatment, but I accepted it and looked forward to our plans to get together during the summer, after my chemo treatments were over.

The days passed way too fast, and, before I knew it, it was time for me to return to the CTCA.

# Chapter Fourteen

The morning I was getting ready to leave for the CTCA, Todd kissed me goodbye and left for work. Nate and Courtney got ready and left for school on the bus. My neighbor Lois would come for Jenna at 11:00, and Amy was going to pick me up to take me to the CTCA. I got in the shower, and as I began to wash my hair, a huge clump of it came out in my hand. And then another. Rather than having some patches of hair and some bald spots, I made an on-the-spot decision to "go all bald." I got more shampoo and kept scrubbing and shedding. Hair was sticking to my wet skin. Water began to rise in the tub, as hair clogged the drain. I was traumatized.

Tears ran down my cheeks, as hair, mixed with shampoo and water, ran down my body. I began to sing praises to God. He alone knew how I was feeling. I had been dreading this moment. I knew it was coming, but I never imagined my hair would all come out in one washing! I had asked Jodi how it was to lose your hair a second time. She had forewarned me that, as difficult as it is to believe, it is actually harder emotionally to lose your hair the second time than the first! She was right.

I was all alone with God...and the baby who had discovered where I was because of my singing. Jenna had crawled in the bathroom and was crying at the shower curtain for my attention. I sang louder. She cried louder. I cried harder. So did she. Finally, I realized she would not be put off any longer, so I turned off the shower and opened the curtain. "We'll finish this later, God," I said out loud. I stepped out, wrapped a towel around me, and scooped up Jenna. She stopped crying and stared at me with a puzzled look. "I can only imagine what Mommy must look like right now!" I said to her.

Jenna eventually fell asleep in my arms. After laying her in the crib, I went back into the bathroom. I shut the door, conscientiously trying to avoid the mirror. As I leaned down to scoop all the hair from the tub into a plastic bag, I prayed, "Lord, You know how very hard this is for me, yet You have allowed it to happen to me not once, but twice. Please give me the strength to handle being bald again. I know You love me, and I know you are here with me now. Please help me."

Just then I happened to glance at the mirror. And I saw quite a sight – a combination of clumps of hair still attached to my head, detached hair sticking to my head, and varying sized bald spots. I stared at the image in the mirror. I was stunned.

After unclogging the drain, I stepped back into the shower. I once again began to sing, as I proceeded to wash the rest of the hair off of my head. As bald as a cue ball, I got out of the shower, dried off with a fresh towel, and cleaned up the rest of the hair from the tub. I tied up the bag tightly, and put it deep into the kitchen trash. I was going to be gone for a week, which was hard enough on Courtney.

Not wanting her to find clumps of my hair everywhere, I systematically destroyed all the evidence of my unsettling morning.

Several hours later, Amy and I were at the CTCA, and I was once again undergoing chemo. We stayed at a hotel, and daily went to the hospital for my five-hour treatment. Some days I felt well enough to go to the beach for a few minutes, other days I only had the strength to crawl in bed. Amy was accommodating and gracious, somehow managing to give me dignity in spite of my looks, state, and circumstances.

When I returned home later that week, I was so sick that I couldn't get out of bed. My heart yearned to be with my family, but my body wouldn't cooperate. I began to get more and more dehydrated as my body rejected my feeble attempts to eat or drink. I ended up in the hospital to be treated for dehydration.

Two treatments down, four to go. This was going to be another long haul.

# Chapter Fifteen

Understandably, depression is common among cancer patients. For some, it is so severe that they can't get out of bed. For others, it's a low-level sadness, like a cloud hanging over their heads. The month after I was first diagnosed with cancer, without warning, I began to have suicidal thoughts. I was incredibly frightened. I immediately called Todd and he called Dr. Hanse, who immediately put me on a low dose of an antidepressant. Although the antidepressant took care of the depression, I soon began to struggle with something else.

From time to time, a panic attack would strike. The first time it happened, I was home alone. I broke out in a sweat, my hands began to shake uncontrollably, and I became light-headed. At first I had trouble breathing, but then, when I overcompensated, I began to hyperventilate. With tears streaming down my face, I called Todd and he came home from work immediately. The episode lasted over an hour, and left me exhausted. Dr. Hanse prescribed an anti-anxiety medication. The medication helped, but I still had many similar attacks.

Our medical expenses continued to grow. I felt like such a burden. At least my business was bringing in some income, even though I was unable to work. (God, knowing our needs before we knew them, had allowed me to establish my business that continued to produce an income during the many months I was unable to work.) But I felt badly for Todd. In order to help with medical bills, he was taking any overtime work he could find. But those opportunities were rare, and we felt very much at the mercy of God.

God, in a myriad of ways, always provided our needs. When my dryer broke, my grandma bought me a new one. My aunts and uncles, who are on fixed incomes themselves, often sent us checks. Our church family gave us another large financial gift. Through all of them, as well as many other friends and relatives, all of our needs were met.

My mom took me to the CTCA for my next round of chemo. Dr. Benson, the psychiatrist, met with me to find out how I was doing emotionally. He talked me through several issues, adjusted my meds based on my recent anxiety attacks, and released me to finish the week of chemo. During the rest of the week, I saw the nutritionist, the naturopath, the oncologist, the physical therapy team, and hosts of others as I completed my third of six prescribed rounds of chemo.

When that week was finally over and I was back home, the side effects once again spiraled out of control. This time the symptoms not only forced me to spend still another night in the emergency room, they also landed me back in the office of my oncologist, Dr. Hanse. He had been receiving all the updates from the CTCA, and, after reviewing my symptoms, he recommended eliminating one of the two chemo drugs and substituting a lower dose of a different drug. These would be administered once a week for the next three weeks only, and then I would be done. He offered to administer the chemo at his office in Lafayette, which is much closer, and then suggested that I think it over and discuss it with my doctors from the CTCA before making a decision.

I continued to be in touch with Jodi. She called one day to tell me this story. Rick took her to the emergency room one evening when her body was trying to pass a kidney stone. Kidney stones were commonplace for Jodi, but this time she had symptoms of sepsis – 105° fever, jaundice, swelling, and excruciating pain. The doctors determined that surgery, to blast the stone into smaller pieces that her body could expel, was necessary. But they warned Jodi that her heart might stop during surgery. They were, in fact, amazed that it hadn't already stopped. Not only could they not assure her that the surgery would be successful, they doubted that she would live through it.

God worked a miracle that day. He used the doctors and team of technicians to save Jodi's life. The surgery was successful, but she came down with a staph infection afterwards. As she was settled into her room for recovery, a nurse came in to check her stats. Jodi described the nurse to me, "Lori, she was so grumpy! She handled me so gruffly. I just started crying in my heart to God. I confess, I was having a pity party, but I just said to Him, 'God, I've had a rough evening here. I am okay that I had a kidney stone and surgery, and even that I now have a staph infection, but God, could I at least have a nice nurse?'"

Even as she was praying, the Holy Spirit convicted her and she began to look at the nurse through eyes of compassion. She realized that in order for that nurse to be so insensitive, she must have had a hard life. Jodi's heart went out to her, and despite her pain, she began to talk to her – about her work, about her family. When she asked "Do you have any kids?" Jodi sensed a slight softening of the woman's heart.

The woman said that she had five children, to which Jodi responded, "What a coincidence! So do I! Two of mine are in heaven, and three are here."

The woman looked at Jodi with obvious interest in spite of her detached facial expression, and said flatly, "All five of mine are adopted. I can't have children because I've had 18 abortions."

"Wow! That's another thing we have in common! One of my babies in heaven is a result of an abortion that I had before I met Jesus. Jesus has taught me how to live without carrying the guilt of that abortion with me. Would you like to meet my Friend Jesus?"

Tears were now freely flowing down the nurse's cheeks. She nodded, ever so slightly, and Jodi told her of the Jesus she knew so well - of his sacrificial death on a cross so that all of us can live free from sin's guilt.

As Jodi was recounting the story, she said that she had momentarily lost sight of the fact that God has a perfect plan for her life. She was consumed with her own pain and misery, forgetting that God places us in the midst of persons who are suffering because they need the hope that only Jesus can bring.

Once again, I was inspired by Jodi's concern for others in the midst of her own suffering. Her life, a living reflection of God, challenges me to be aware that God purposefully places people in my path who need to hear of His love.

Before Jodi and I hung up that day, I told her the dates of my next chemo appointment at the CTCA. She and Rick were considering meeting us there. I got excited. I dreaded going for treatment, but seeing Jodi would brighten that considerably.

I continued to suffer serious side effects from the chemo treatment, so Todd and I decided that I should talk with the staff of the CTCA about Dr. Hanse's recommendations to lessen the dosage and shorten the treatment time. I planned to do that when I made my fourth trip to the CTCA. I also expected to have a chemo treatment. My friend Amy took me for the appointment. Our plan was that she would stay a few days, and then another friend, Sue, would come for the rest of the week and take me home. After checking in at the hospital, I met with Dr. Morgan, the oncologist. I told him what Dr. Hanse had recommended because of the severe side effects I continued to experience. After reviewing my records, he agreed with Dr. Hanse's recommendations, and offered for me to finish the treatments in Lafayette. He then released me to go home, but I opted to stay long enough to keep my scheduled appointments with other staff members.

At one point, I was well enough to make an appointment with the person in charge of the CT department. It was extremely traumatic for me to relive my experience with the harsh technician (whose identity I did not reveal), and even harder to tell Jodi's story. She had given me permission to share it, because we both desired to see changes in that department so future patients wouldn't have to suffer as we had. The CT department head was very receptive; she thanked me many times for coming in to see her, and acted on the information immediately by calling an emergency meeting of all department heads. I was, frankly, quite impressed.

As planned, Amy went home and Sue arrived. The next morning, she took me in for my appointment with Dr. Benson, the psychiatrist. He once again recalibrated my meds and we talked in depth about my emotional well-being. Mostly, I just wanted to be done with cancer once and for all. But it would be some time before that wish came true.

I was home a few days before I went to Dr. Hanse's office in Lafayette for another round of chemo. As it turned out, it was my last. Once again, the side effects were almost more than my frail body could endure. After still another visit to the emergency room, the doctor decided that enough was enough. In his words, "We don't want to 'kill you with kindness.'" Too much of a good thing (chemo to eradicate the cancer) was turning out to be a bad thing (damage to my body). I was relieved beyond words. I could now begin to rebuild my body, and try to put the fractured pieces of my life back together. I knew it would be a long haul before I was anything like my former self, and I knew that some of the chemo damage to my body was permanent, but, at long last, I was free from cancer! In church a few Sundays later, I shared this testimony:

> I stand before you today in remission from cancer. These last ten months have been quite an experience! Cancer waged a war for my life, and it won several battles along the way, but ultimately, God won the war.

Cancer took my hair...twice. God used it to humble me to the very core of myself, showing me that true worth lies not on the outside, but on who I have been made on the inside, through Christ.

Cancer put my life on hold for ten long months, robbing me of the very basic experience of being a wife, mother, daughter, sister, friend, and business leader.

Cancer left me scared, broken, fearful, and weak.

God showed me that at my worst, He was at His best...doing a work in and through me – ultimately resulting in many lives touched and reached for the Kingdom.

Cancer temporarily stole my happiness.

God restored my hope, reminding me that true joy is found only in Him.

Cancer gave me pain.

God gave me comfort, protection, and assurance of a heavenly place He is preparing for me where I will no longer hurt.

Praise God!! For the ultimate victory is His!! I wouldn't trade these last ten months for anything.

My doctors tell me that the probability of cancer returning in my lifetime is 75-80%. The first two years are when it will most likely reappear if, indeed, God deems it so. My odds of recurrence decrease as time goes on, but I will always be predisposed to cancer and have to watch my exercise, diet, and lifestyle carefully. But in the end, it's up to God whether or not we will revisit this disease.

I will always live with a black cloud over my head and the possibility that it could rain at any time. But for now, I choose to look up and say, "Today it is not raining." God has given me today. I am thankful. I will not waste it.

LJM
July, 2003

I was in remission for the first time in almost a year. This is what we had been fighting for. We were very grateful to God!

# Chapter Sixteen

"Life in remission" took on a meaning of its own. As I attempted to return to my previous responsibilities and routine, my life seemed far from normal. Nate and Courtney had completed a school year. Jenna had started developmental therapy to improve her speech and motor skills. Todd was preparing to buy the business at which he was currently employed. As for me, I had so much catching up to do! But my body, a frail imitation of its former self, refused to fully cooperate.

I was able to go back to work. It took a lot of effort to juggle business demands, keep up with my older kids' active schedules, and care for Jenna. But, gradually, I increased the hours that I spent at work. With my focus on reclaiming my life, I didn't notice that I was neglecting my body.

In the meantime, Jodi and Rick came to visit. Although still battling cancer, she was feeling somewhat better. We shopped, talked, and played. Our families got to know each other and our daughters, Courtney and Kaitlyn, particularly bonded.

Jodi was a great help as I tried to figure out how to integrate my former and current lives. She also joined my Mary Kay team. We had one more excuse to stay in touch.

Three months passed way too quickly, and I was once again making plans to go to the CTCA for my quarterly evaluation. My scans had already been done at the local hospital. The doctor had declared me still in remission (what a relief) and had sent the results ahead to the CTCA. As usual, I had appointments with the nutritionist, the naturopath, the oncologist, and the psychiatrist, Dr Benson. The last one was the appointment that changed my life drastically.

It all started so innocently. Dr. Benson was making some dosage changes for my medication, and needed to know my weight. A nurse took me to another room to weigh, and, as usual, I stepped onto the scale backwards. (I had learned from my past struggles with anorexia to purposefully avoid seeing how much I weighed.) I heard Dr. Benson and the nurse conferring. They asked me to step off the scale for a minute. I did. Then they asked me to step back on. I did. After more shuffling of papers and conferring, Dr. Benson and I went back into his office.

"Lori, just out of curiosity, do you mind if I ask you how much you think you weigh?" he asked.

"I really have no idea. Before I got cancer, I weighed about 123. I know I have lost weight because my clothes are loose, and I see the changes in my body."

"If you were to guess, what number would you give me?" he asked.

I had to think about it. I knew I had lost weight through the ovarian cancer deal, but then my appetite had improved and I had eaten well, I thought, for several weeks prior to my next surgery. "Probably 105-108 pounds," I said.

"Would you be upset if I told you it was lower than that?" he countered.

"Okay, 102," I said.

"Lower still."

"100?" I was beginning to get alarmed by the look on his face and this line of questioning. There was no way that I weighed less than 100 pounds!

"Lori, I don't want to upset you by telling you the actual number of pounds you weigh, but I need you to know you are dangerously thin." Dr. Benson said.

"Under 100?" I asked, disbelief in my voice.

"Yes. Even under 90," he said, measuring my response very carefully.

I gasped. I had no idea I was that thin. "I think you had better tell me the number," I said when I could breathe again.

"Are you sure?" he asked, respectful of my past history. I nodded.

"Lori, you weigh 84 pounds." Tears began to stream down my face. I was in shock. I tried to counter with an answer, but none came. I looked down at my body like it had betrayed me. I had no idea I had done such damage to my body. I was scared. And it got still worse.

"I need you to understand how critical this is," Dr. Benson said, once again choosing his words carefully. "I am actually shocked that you have not had a heart attack. Even at 90 pounds you would be at high risk for that. But this low..." His voice trailed off and he shook his head incredulously. "Lori, you must not do any strenuous exercise or activity. You must not run. You must not vacuum. You must not lift your daughter or a load of laundry. Until you gain some weight, your heart is our biggest concern. I cannot stress enough how important it is for you to take it easy. I will be in touch with your oncologist, Dr. Morgan, as well as your nutritionist. Do I have your permission to share with them your history of anorexia as well as what we found out today?"

I nodded. I was not only in shock but incredibly frightened. In all the years I had struggled with my weight, I had never been below 99 pounds, much less in the low 80's. My mind went to my family. Poor Todd had endured so much with me and my struggles with anorexia in the early years of our marriage. How could I tell him this? And, what about my parents? This was embarrassing and overwhelming. But here sat Dr. Benson telling me to get a grip on it, or die of a heart attack.

Oddly, I had come to terms with the possibility of dying from cancer. But a heart attack? As I sat there attempting to absorb what I was being told, I got mad. Not at Dr. Benson or anyone else. I was mad at the cancer. Cancer had already taken so much from me; it had no right to put me at risk for a heart attack. I was determined to not let it attack still another part of my health.

In the long run, being told that I weighed 84 pounds was a blessing in disguise. I left his office determined to slow down, eat, and gain weight! This was an opposite of my typical response to a crisis. Normally, in order to regain the control I felt was losing, I would not eat, perpetuating the seemingly unending cycle of anorexia.

As I had anticipated, when I told him about my weight, Todd was badly shaken. I carefully avoided strenuous activity and I began to "push through" feelings of being out of control. I tried to eat as much and as healthily as I could. And I gained a few pounds.

We later learned what no one had suspected at the time: the scale on which I was weighed at the CTCA was not calibrated correctly, and I actually had weighed 98, rather than 84, pounds. I believe that God used human error to snap me back to my senses and to fight harder to live.

That summer I was able to go to my annual business seminar in Dallas and thoroughly enjoyed my time there. Also, my brother Kevin's family came to Indiana from Mexico for the summer, and my sister Gayle's family came from the west coast for a week. We were at my parents' home for a few days – the first time our entire family had been together since my cancer diagnosis over a year before.

Realizing this time with my family was priceless, I devised a plan. I purchased small gifts for each family member and wrote individual thank you letters to my husband, my children, and my parents, as well as my siblings and their spouses. After supper one night, with all of us together, I was able to express in words the gratitude flowing from my heart. Before sharing with each of them individually, I addressed them all:

"What a journey this has been! The last ten months have been full of surprises and ups and downs as we have traveled together my journey with cancer. There are truly no words to sum up my feelings that would fully encompass the experience. But I'd like to try to express to you my deepest gratitude to you, my family, who have ridden this roller coaster with me. I have seen first-hand the place I hold in each of your hearts as you have shown me by your actions how much you love me."

My gift to my parents was the sitting fee for a family portrait, which still hangs on the wall in my parents' home. Every time I see it, I'm reminded of God's goodness. He allowed me to go through cancer, but He also allowed me to live.

I realized anew that, with all my heart, living is what I desired to do.

# Chapter Seventeen

Looking back, I realized there was definitely a pattern of how my life was being lived. The focal point had become my quarterly evaluations. The doctors had told me that the probability of my cancer recurring was 75%. So, I had an evaluation, got a clean report, and then lived at full speed until my next evaluation drew near. Nervous about the pending results, I had fewer and fewer functions in my date book. I refused to fill my appointment book with work-related activities, because I didn't want to have to cancel them if the prognosis from my next scan was bad. Instead, I filled my days with "busy work" to keep my mind occupied. I told my mom I would bake some cookies for our family holiday celebration. Two dozen cookies turned into 35 dozen! I decided to decorate my house, and so I bought a few trees to go with the ones I already had. Then a few more...until I had 21 trees! And I hung lights–everywhere! I didn't realize how out of control I had gotten until Todd pointed it out to me in mid-October.

"Lori," he said, "It takes you ten minutes every night to unplug all the lights before you come to bed! I can't get hamburger out of the freezer without moving a dozen containers of cookies! You have every present purchased, wrapped, and under the tree. What are you running from? Why are you expending all your energy in such silly ways, yet you refuse to hold an appointment with your business because you are so afraid you will have to cancel it if your tests results come back cancerous? You need to get a grip! You need to live now – not between the cracks of your evaluations! I am tripping over trees and trimmings! Please see this for what it is, and fix it before I am living in a forest!"

Gradually I got the point. Previously, in a hospital room with Jodi, God had shown me that life was not meant to be put on hold pending scan results, but was rather meant to be lived to the fullest every day. I was chastised in my heart and determined to do better at living each day and, as the Bible instructs, rejoicing and being glad.viii I was scheduled to sing again at church, and this is the testimony I shared at that time:

> Tomorrow I go in for a CT scan, and Wednesday we will find out if cancer has re-entered my body.
>
> One year and two months ago, I first heard the dreaded word "cancer" as it pertained to me. Ten months later, I had been through a diagnosis of ovarian cancer and colon cancer, three surgeries, seven rounds of chemotherapy, six trips to the emergency room as side effects wracked my body, four CT scans, a PET scan, and more IV's and needles than even I could keep track of.
>
> Then in May, we heard the blessed words "in remission," and I proceeded to reclaim my life by desperately trying to regain some semblance of control–regrouping what

my life had been before it got "thrown into the blender," so to speak.

But I had not taken into account the very real toll that ten months of fighting cancer had taken on my body. For starters, I have lost over 20 pounds. Because of that alone, I have a weakened heart and can't even vacuum the house without the possibility of having a heart attack. I also have been very fatigued, and have a condition called "chemo brain," which has left me with very pathetic short term memory – a fact to which many of you can attest! So the sum total of all of these effects showed me that I was trying to live the life God had given to my "before-cancer body," when in fact I need to realize I am only to be faithful to live the life He has given me with my "in-remission body," which at this point has to be far less active.

I have also learned through all of this – even as I face another evaluation this week – God has the power and control over my life whether the diagnosis is "cancer has returned" or "you are still in remission." Like the well-known song says, "Sometimes, He calms the storm, but other times He calms His child."[ix] Of course, I desire for the storm to blow over this time, but I cling to His promises to stay with me and see me through, no matter what Wednesday brings. And I pray that, whatever the outcome, He will receive the glory."

LJM
November 5, 2003

God granted me a happy Christmas. My test results once again came back negative, and I was able to enjoy the holidays knowing I was still in remission.

In early January each year, I go to a conference in South Bend, Indiana with my Mary Kay group. I was asked to speak on behalf of the Mary Kay Ash Charitable Foundation, which had been established, in part, for cancer research. I had managed to speak at the conference the previous year, 2003, while Todd was in China and I was in remission from my ovarian cancer. Both times, it was an honor to be asked. But this year was especially important to me, because Rick and Jodi were coming from Wisconsin for the conference. Jodi had worked her way to the top in my unit, and was to be recognized for her achievements. I was so proud of her.

I told my story and asked for help to raise funds for fighting this horrible disease called cancer. The year before, we had raised over $10,000, and this year it was more than $12,000. I was doing this for all the people who hadn't had cancer yet, for those of us who had cancer and were in remission, and for my friend Jodi, who was still very much fighting the battle. We had a very special conference that year, and I was doubly blessed – to be feeling as well as I was, and to have Jodi there with me.

About that time, Jodi began to seek in earnest a new treatment facility, as her breast cancer was growing rapidly. She found a doctor in Chicago, and started having treatments there. Occasionally, after her treatment they would come down to our Indiana farm to see us; we visited them in Wisconsin as often as possible. When we weren't together in person, Jodi and I stayed in touch by phone.

My quarterly evaluations became routine, and I was able to forget about them until a week or so beforehand. I would get a little stressed, but so far God had blessed me with good reports. I began to feel like we had beaten the odds and, even though the doctors were carefully checking everything and still expecting something to show up, I felt like I had been freed from the burden of cancer once and for all. I had truly begun to live again, and things were good. I had many speaking engagements, and was able to share all God had taught me through my journey with cancer.

When we were at the CTCA for one of my evaluations, Rick and Jodi came to be with us. We had such a great time together – especially because neither she nor I were in treatment, and my test results once again came back negative. I continued to be blessed and honored by Rick and Jodi's friendship!

Another time that I went for an evaluation, I took Courtney with me. After we had finished the rounds of meeting with the doctors and the rest of the staff, we decided to go out and enjoy the beach. I noticed that people were staring at me as we made our way to the water's edge. As I was lying on the beach, I heard a passersby whispering, and saw them looking at my body with curious glances. I looked down and saw that my legs were covered in bruises and looked horrible! I vowed to keep my legs and arms covered until they were healed, which was several months later.

Although I was no longer on any medication for anxiety, I was still on the antidepressant drug which I had been taking for 2½ years. My doctor agreed when I asked to be weaned off of it. Three weeks later, I was no longer taking the medication. Great plan, with only one little kink.

I was not well enough to go to church with Todd and the kids that evening. I was relaxing on the couch when I was hit with the worst anxiety attack ever! I began to shake uncontrollably. My body got clammy and my breathing was erratic. I started to see spots everywhere. I locked the door – I was afraid of my own shadow. I was totally devoid of energy, but the spots on the carpet were driving me to distraction, and I needed to keep busy or go crazy by myself in a house full of shadows. I got the carpet cleaner and brush and I sat weakly on the floor and began to scrub at those spots. I also began to sing praise songs at the top of my lungs to drive away the shadows.

Nate was the first one in the house. I saw him and stopped singing and scrubbing and collapsed in a heap. "Thank God, you're home!" I said, and then began to cry inconsolably.

"Dad!" Nate yelled.

Todd came into the house and assessed the situation. I clung to him, unwilling to let him out of my sight. He held me and motioned to Nate and Courtney to take Jenna upstairs. He eased himself out of my vice-like grip to get to the phone and call my sister Gayle, who is a nurse. I couldn't stand being alone, but I had no strength left in me. With all I could muster, I crawled to the bottom of the stairs so I could hear the voices of my children. Todd reappeared with a bottle of Benadryl© and a piece of cake.

"Honey, I need you to take this medicine and eat this," he said. I realized that I was the one who was "wacked out," but at that moment I looked at him like he was crazy! Benadryl© and cake were supposed to drive away the shadows and get rid of the spots? Who was the crazy one here? Having no strength to argue, I complied. After I finished the Benadryl© and cake, he helped me upstairs and put me in a warm bath. After ten minutes or so, he gently dressed me in my pajamas, helped me into bed, and held me until I fell asleep.

I awakened the next morning to the sounds of Todd helping the kids get ready for school. I lay there for awhile to assess my condition. I actually felt pretty good. No shadows, no overactive imagination, no spots, and my heart was no longer racing. Okay, maybe the wacky prescription had done the trick after all!

After the kids left for school, I asked Todd the question begging to be asked. "What was with the cake and the Benadryl©?" He explained that's what Gayle prescribed when she realized that I was sleep deprived and my blood sugar levels were low. Although it seemed strange at the time, I can't complain about the results.

Two years passed ... Evaluations, life with family, health "hiccups," like bladder and kidney infections, anxiety attacks (although increasingly more infrequent), business matters, times with Jodi. And it was good. Then I had an evaluation, and, once again, my life was about to be "thrown into a blender."

The cancer had returned.

# Chapter Eighteen

Why it surprised me, I don't know. The doctors had all warned me it was a very real possibility. But when I went in for my June 2005 evaluation, and Dr. Hanse said I had a spot on my lung that looked like cancer, I sat there in shocked disbelief. He told me I had several choices. First choice: wait a few months until the spot was larger, do a needle biopsy to confirm that it was indeed cancerous, and then have surgery to remove it. Second choice: have a PET scan to definitively diagnose the spot, and then have surgery to remove it. Third choice: just go ahead and have the surgery. From where I sat, all roads led to surgery. I am not a procrastinator. My thought was that if I had to have surgery, I wanted to get it over with.

Dr. Hanse wanted to do a Positron Emission Tomography (PET) scan to be more certain that the spot was cancer before he put me through a very painful, invasive surgery. That made sense to me. If the spot glowed, it was most likely cancerous. It glowed. Dr. Hanse assured me that if they got it all when they did the surgery, I would not have to go through chemo again. My relief regarding not having to have chemo was so great that I was tending to look past the surgery.

Yet again, I was scheduled to sing at church, and this is what I shared:

> Seems like it hasn't been that long ago I was up here sharing with you all about the latest medical crisis I was about to face.
>
> Well, here we go again! But I go in this time with another weapon in my arsenal: even greater confidence in the faithfulness of my Heavenly Father. You see, rather recently He carried me through some pretty tough times, and He has never left me nor forsaken me.[x] I have walked through the very valley of the shadow of death – more than once – and He has been my constant companion.[xi] I found that as I have drawn near to Him, He has drawn near to me.xii And if He sees and cares for a single sparrow, how much more is he caring for me, His child?[xiii]
>
> I prayed a prayer, "God, about this spot on my lung...will You just touch it and heal it and let that be that?" And He said, "No, Lori, that's not My plan for you this time. You have to walk through this, and I will be with you every step."
>
> So I prayed, "Okay, but after we get rid of the spot with this surgery, if it's cancerous, can we skip the whole chemo thing this time? I really, really don't want to go through that again!" And God said, "Yes! We can forgo chemo. That you don't have to face right now."

Then I prayed once more, "Now, when we get this all done and behind us ...can this be the end of the surgery/cancer business for me once and for all?" He answered, "My child – I know the plans I have for you[xiv] – you will just have to wait and see on that one. But trust in this: I am holding you very tenderly at this time."

LJM
July 24, 2005

Dr. Hanse referred me to Dr. Seers, who specializes in lung surgery. His first words to me I will never forget. He said, "Lori, I will not lie to you. Lung surgery is the most painful surgery a body can go through. The organ we will be working on, and quite possibly removing, is one that you use at least 30 times a minute to stay alive."

He then went on to explain the surgery he would perform. First, he would make an incision about 18 inches long to remove my fifth rib. After that, he would cut through the muscle and nerve tissue between my ribs to gain access to the lower lobe of my left lung. He would remove the offending cancerous-looking spot, and send it to pathology, while I lay on the operating table. It would take about 30 minutes to get the report back from pathology. If the report showed that it was cancer, he would remove the rest of the lobe. If it wasn't cancer, he would just stitch me back up. The recovery period would be long, and I would have a lot of pain. "Any questions?" he asked.

I had one. "Can you put my rib back?"

He looked perplexed. Why was I asking that question? "No, they will also send the rib to pathology to determine if the cancer is in your bones."

"But," I stammered. "After that then, can I at least have it back in a jar?"

Again, he was a little puzzled by my question. "Lori, we are doing what we can to help save your life. You will be undergoing a major, painful surgery. In the larger scheme of things, your rib plays a minor role."

I began to cry. Not because I was about to undergo another major surgery and have to go through recovery again. Not because I once again had cancer, and had to face major issues with that. But, because once again, cancer was taking something from me. I had not expected this, and I had not given my permission! I felt like I was running out of "disposable parts," and if they begin adding bones to my short list, then there would be no end to my surgeries. I could live without the organs they had removed during the hysterectomy and colon surgeries. I could live without the lower lobe of my lung. (We hoped.) But this was the first time they told me they were going to be removing one of my bones and not putting it back. The lung, they could have. The bone, well, it wasn't on my list. I was shaken.

On the way home from the doctor, I told Todd that I was really upset about this rib thing. It reminded me of how I had felt the previous summer when I had been told, during the process of renewing my driver's license, that I could not be an organ donor. Chemotherapy had disqualified me. And my family voted against other posthumous possibilities I considered! I just die and I'm buried. No heroics. When it's over, it's over. I was in a funk.

Now I was in somewhat of the same mindset over this rib business. I called my Daddy, who always understood my problems, gave me good advice, and got through to my heart. He told me to quit looking at cancer as this big ugly thing that was taking things from me. Instead, he advised, I should look at it as an opportunity to learn, to grow, to become more like Christ, and ultimately to weed out things that aren't of eternal significance...like my pink Cadillac that represented my Mary Kay accomplishments, like the little heart on my driver's license that said I'm an organ donor, and even like my rib. I have since come to terms with reality. But it doesn't change my ever-shrinking list of expendable parts!

We scheduled the surgery, and I got my affairs in order at home, including setting up a schedule for Jenna's care by making a color-coded chart. It was a long two months, but Jenna held her own and made lots of friends! I suppose it's no different than people whose kids go to childcare every day. But for me it was unfamiliar and unsettling, and I so wanted to be the one caring for this precious gift from the other side of the world! But so many loving people – Stacy, Mary, Tammy, Kelly, Aunt Amy, Aunt Tammy, Machelle, and Jennifer got to enjoy her, and I knew she was in great hands!

Again, the people from our church set up a schedule for bringing meals to us and cleaning our house. Someone even did our laundry for us. Once again, we realized how very blessed we were!

Meanwhile, unbeknown to me, in the wee hours of the morning prior to my surgery, my friend Jodi in Wisconsin was having a rough night due to her pain from cancer. The Lord prompted her to get out of bed and pen the following prayer, which I didn't receive until later.

> Lord, my sleep is very restless. So I'll pray for Lori, my dear friend. Lord, I ask and believe in Your angels to sur-

round her with love and peace. I pray a blessing of healing over Lori from her mind through her heart, penetrating her spirit and following through her body in Jesus' Name. Thank You for answering this prayer.

I also pray for a new song to rise up in her heart! Let everything that has breath praise Your Name! Jesus, Your Name is worthy to be praised.

I ask that Lori not only make it thorough this surgery, but she makes it through with never having another bout with cancer again. May her faith be at a position it has never been before and may she quickly arise to receive it with her spirit. I love my friend and her family and am not so willing to lose her.

In Jesus' Name, hallelujah! Praise the almighty King! He is worthy Amen.

Jodi Lind
July 27, 2005

I needed Jodi's prayers that day. It was surreal to be back in a hospital gown with a little cap on my head, the technicians all around, and the doctors once again coming into my cubicle to tell me what was going to happen. It seemed as if cancer had a grip on my life, and it wouldn't set me free. Predictably, I had a "here-we-go-again" feeling. As before, all the doctors and Todd circled my bed and prayed. I looked at Dr. Seers and asked him a question that I had wanted to ask for some time. "Are all the surgeons in your group Christians?"

"Yes, we all are," he responded. "In fact, we are thinking about hiring a Jew so we can all take off on Christmas!" he quipped. Todd and I couldn't help but chuckle as Dr. Seers exited the cubicle to go scrub.

I spent our 18th anniversary in the Intensive Care Unit. Todd bought me a dozen beautiful pink roses, but I couldn't have them in my room until I was moved from the ICU.

As I woke up from surgery, I heard a gurgling sound. I didn't give it much thought as I drifted in and out of consciousness. Visitors were restricted to family only, and I didn't even remember that they had come. Those first days were a total blur.

About four days after the surgery, I was coherent enough to understand what had transpired. The pathology report showed that the spot was cancerous, so Dr. Seers removed the entire lower lobe of my left lung. Pain medication was injected, two tubes were inserted, and the incision was closed. The tubes were draining fluid from around my lung as it was healing. Thus, the "gurgling" sound. And here I was thinking maybe there was a fish aquarium behind me.

Four days had passed, but the real work of healing was just beginning. When they weaned me from some of the heavier pain meds, I was totally unprepared for how much I would be hurting. Even rolling over so that the hospital staff could change my sheets was an extremely painful ordeal with two tubes protruding from my left side.

Five days after surgery I was moved from the ICU into another room, where I would remain for five more days. As the doctors decreased my pain medication dosage, the pain increased. By the time I was released to go home, I understood the battle ahead. I had to do breathing exercises that burned my lung. I had to walk a certain distance each day to continue to stretch my lung capacity. As the muscles that were cut during surgery were healing, pain ripped through my body, sending tears streaming down my face. I experienced two months of intense pain. I was in the midst of another very long battle.

The healing process was hindered on one occasion when I tangled with a couple of goats. I was the loser in my attempt to keep them out of the flowers I had planted around our house. The energy I expended trying to get them into the barn left me in a lot of pain, and landed me back at the doctor's office. He said I had torn some of the muscle tissue that was not yet healed, and he extended my pain medication.

In late September of 2005, Todd and I went to the Bahamas to celebrate our anniversary, something we had wanted to do for three years. I was weak and frail and still in a significant amount of pain, but I didn't let that stop me from having a good time. The hurricane season, however, kept the weather overcast, windy, and chilly the whole time we were there. I vote for a trip redo!

# Chapter Nineteen

We had made plans with Rick and Jodi to meet them at the Wisconsin Dells in October of that same year. But because Jodi had taken a sharp turn for the worse, our trip was cancelled. Instead, Courtney, Todd, and I decided to drive to their home in Wisconsin to spend a few days with them.

Before we even got there, Jodi was back in the hospital. I went in to see her. She didn't look like my friend Jodi. Her face was all puffy from steroids and pain killers, and she was pasty and weak. She was sleeping when I got to her room, so I just sat by her bedside, held her hand, and prayed. During the previous months, she had alluded to the fact that the doctors had told her she had cancer throughout her body, and the illness was terminal. I knew all of that intellectually, but seeing her now, in this condition, made it all too real. I couldn't bear to think of losing this dear friend. But I now knew that I would probably need to find the strength to say goodbye soon.

She woke up. Because of the pain medication, it took her a little while to take in her surroundings. When she finally saw me, tears began to stream down her face. "This isn't how it was supposed to be," she whispered hoarsely. I nodded my agreement and silently wept with her.

I spent the next two days by Jodi's bedside, while Todd and Courtney hung out with Jodi's husband Rick and her daughter Kaitlyn. I was no stranger to hospital rooms, to be sure, nor was I a stranger to being in a hospital room with Jodi. But this was wrong. I was supposed to be in the bed next to hers, not walking around cancer-free. Why had God chosen to see me through three cancers, while my dear friend Jodi was fighting to survive the first? My heart hurt so badly I thought it would break. I put on a brave face for Jodi, and we were able to spend some priceless time together. But when we left the hospital and returned home to Indiana, I left a piece of my heart in Wisconsin. It felt like I was saying goodbye to my precious friend for the last time here on earth. Courtney and I sobbed for the next two hours as we headed home.

Over the course of the next few weeks, Jodi was in and out of the hospital. She kept me posted on her condition over the phone as best she could, but her speech became harder and harder to understand. The doctors were trying to "keep her comfortable," and she had so many pain killers in her system that one day she fell asleep while I was talking to her on the phone! The doctors gave her until the holidays to live. In typical Jodi fashion, she defied their predictions and had a great Christmas.

As always, January brought with it not only cold weather, but also my annual Mary Kay trip to South Bend to speak for the Mary Kay Ash Charitable Foundation. Jodi had given her permission, and I shared her story.

Exactly one year ago on the first night of Jamboree, a young lady named Jodi was standing in the wings, ready to go on stage to be recognized for being an Emerald Star Consultant. The wonderful Kendra Cross was also over there as a "stage hand" – directing traffic, so to speak. She approached Jodi and gave her a hug, congratulating her on her success. Then she stood back and casually remarked that she liked Jodi's hair. In typical fashion, Jodi replied, "Thank you, it's a wig." At Kendra's shocked look, Jodi quickly added, "I have breast cancer."

Kendra's eyes welled up in tears as she took Jodi's hands in hers and said, "I am so sorry. Whose unit are you in?" Jodi only had a quick moment before going on stage. She quickly replied, "Lori Miller's," then hopped up the stairs for her time in the limelight.

Jodi went home to Wisconsin, but made eight more trips to Chicago for chemotherapy. Then, in April, when they thought they had the cancer under control, she was given the devastating news. A new strain of breast cancer had invaded her body. This strain was so aggressive that, if left unchecked, it would actually begin to grow on the outside of her skin. And it soon did. In May, she began to experience more pain than ever before. The last week of June, while we were all busily wrapping up another Mary Kay seminar year, she was hospitalized for what she thought was gallbladder problems. Instead, the cancer was weaving itself around her stomach and other organs. Even so, Jodi finished up her seminar year as #2 in the court of sales, only 50 retail dollars behind the queen in her unit.

As I'm sure you have figured out by now, I am Lori Miller, so proud to say I am the director of this remarkable lady! I met Jodi three years ago as I was walking through an unexpected and very dark time in my life. I had just finished fighting a battle against ovarian cancer, which I won, and six weeks later I was diagnosed with stage 4 colon cancer. I went to Chicago for a second opinion, and that is where Jodi entered my life, my heart, and ultimately, my unit. We have fought the fight against cancer together for several years now. Mine eventually went into remission, only to turn up again this past year – leading to surgery last July to remove a part of my lung where it metastasized. Jodi, on the other hand, has never had the opportunity to say she is in remission, but has bravely battled for more than three years – facing setbacks, unbelievable pain, hospital stays, treatments, side effects, the works. She currently is in the last stages of cancer, in and out of the hospital so often her kids call it "Mommy's hospital." The cancer is running unchecked throughout her body. Lungs, liver, pancreas, stomach, breasts...it is everywhere.

I took a trip to Wisconsin a few weeks ago to spend some time with her. Before I even got there, she was again in the hospital with pneumonia. She was aware of my presence, but unable to acknowledge me as she was so drugged to ease the pain. I sat by her bedside for 1½ days and watched her go in and out of consciousness. When she finally broke through the fog, we had a precious three minutes while she was actually "there." I basically said hello and goodbye before she fell back into her drug-induced sleep.

Jodi will leave behind a husband and three young children. She has had a remarkable influence on so many people just by her vibrant life and love for the Lord. I can release her only because I know she will be in the presence of our Heavenly Father, and she will finally be free of this horrible disease and all the pain it has caused her.

Please fight with me to end cancer once and for all. Jodi should never have to leave this life at age 35. No one should have to go through the pain and misery of cancer. I am privileged to be alive...apparently God isn't finished with me yet. But what about all the Jodi's out there?

We are in a position to do something. As you know, the Mary Kay Ash Charitable Foundation is doing research and making headway into diagnosis and treatment that will help obliterate cancer. It won't come soon enough for Jodi. But you can help make sure someone else isn't affected by cancer – like your mom, sister, best friend, or even yourself. Please give generously. There is a "Jodi" out there you may or may not ever know whose life depends on it. Thank you.

LJM
January, 2006

Jodi surprised us all. In February her condition improved, and she even began to see marked shrinking of her tumors. Even though she was on hospice care, she was once again on a nutritional program that appeared to be working. We continued to call and talk often, even though calls to her were painful from my standpoint. She was always in a "delayed response" mode, and she had a hard time remembering what we were talking about. She was very vague about her health, and it was difficult for me to get an update from her. I now know she just wanted to talk about life and living, not the disease that haunted her. She rose above it time and time again. Her strength and courage amazed me. We even revisited our plans to meet at the Wisconsin Dells. But first, she told me, her family was going on a "trial run" camping trip to see how well she would do.

Their efforts landed her back in the hospital. They had forgotten to take along her pain medication. Later, she told me it was the worse cancer pain to date. Our meeting at Wisconsin Dells was not to be.

In late July, Rick called Todd. He was very shaken and feared the end was near. The nurses said two weeks, tops, was all she had left. He asked if we could please come.

Rick said Jodi was no longer able to speak. I was in shock and denial. I had just spoken to her earlier that month! I hadn't called her for a few weeks, but I had a hard time believing I would never, ever hear her voice again.

We immediately began to make plans to go to Wisconsin. Todd and I were both in a flurry of activity as we prepared to head for Wisconsin as soon as possible. But Rick called back that same day. We were too late.

Jodi was with Jesus.

# Chapter Twenty

Todd and I hurriedly took care of business matters, leaving much in the capable hands of our respective office managers. The next day we hit the road for Wisconsin. Driving up there this time was incredibly hard. As I saw road signs telling us we were approaching Eau Claire, which usually made my heart sing with anticipation of getting nearer to Jodi, my heart began to feel heavier and heavier. I had collapsed into Todd's arms the previous day when Rick called to tell us of her death. I was at once both numb and sharply aware of my loss. By the time we were on our way, I was running on fumes.

As we got closer to our destination, I began to get physically sick to my stomach. I lay down in the back of the truck, and I just prayed and prayed. "God, you know exactly how I am feeling right now. You know how heavy my heart is, and how very much I don't want to be going to Wisconsin to see the body of my dear Jodi. Please give me the strength to make it through these next few days. Make me strong for those kids and for Rick, and even for my Courtney. Take me and somehow use this broken-hearted vessel for Your glory."

I sat up and continued praying silently as I looked over the beautiful Wisconsin hillsides. I continued to commune with God as we rode along, all the time getting closer and closer to...what? An empty place that Jodi used to fill. Her absence would no doubt echo even louder than did her presence.

As I mourned in my heart and prayed to God, I had an urgency to pray for something specific. In obedience, I prayed that whoever was chosen to speak at the funeral would very clearly express the love Jodi had for God and the love she had for her family. I prayed with fervency that these things would be evident at her funeral, honoring her life and her God. I prayed and watched the hillsides go past for at least an hour. Before long, Todd's cell phone rang. He answered it, and from what I overheard, I correctly guessed it was Rick. They talked for a few minutes, and then I heard him say, "I don't know – you will have to ask her." Then he passed the phone to me.

"Lori?" I heard Rick's voice on the other end of the line. "I was wondering if you would be willing to speak at the funeral. I have been thinking about who Jodi would have wanted, and you are the first person who came to mind."

I was stunned! All these hours I was praying specifically for whoever was going to speak at the funeral; now I knew it was going to be me! My response to Rick was "Yes, I would be honored." But in my heart I was crying out to God, "How on earth am I going to get up there and speak? God, you gave me this assignment, and You gave me the heart for what needs to be shared. Now I am just going to trust You for the actual words and the strength to do it."

We went to the hotel first and checked in. I wanted to delay the inevitable as long as possible, but Todd really wanted to get to the house to be with Rick, and Courtney was anxious to see Kaitlyn. Passing the familiar scenery on the way to their house, I wept silently. This place used to be so inviting. After all, I had a dear friend who lit up this part of the world. Now it just felt empty. As we pulled into their driveway, everything looked the same, but felt so different.

I visited for a while with Jodi's parents, Marylou and Jim, who shared a duplex with Rick and Jodi. Jim, who was Jodi's primary caregiver, shared openly about Jodi's last days on earth. One of the stories he told was about his frustration with Jodi because she wouldn't stay in her hospital bed, which was in their side of the duplex. Although the bar on the side of the bed was always up to keep her from falling out and being injured, she could squeeze her small frame through a space at the end of the bar. From time to time, Jim would find her sitting on the floor and would patiently lift her back into the bed, making sure the bar was up and firmly locked. But the next time he checked, she would be on the floor again. Finally, one night, Jim just said, "Okay, Jodi, if you want to be on the floor, I'll just leave you there!" He threw her a pillow and retired for the night.

Later that night five year-old Ciera slipped from the bed where she was sleeping with her daddy. When Rick woke up and looked for her, he found that she had gone to be with her mommy. There he found them – Jodi on the floor with the pillow Jim had thrown her on her lap. Lying on the pillow was little Ciera, sound asleep. Jodi was gently stroking her daughter's hair. Rick took a mental picture of an image he will always carry in his heart before he quietly left the two of them together and headed back to his bedroom.

That was Jodi's final night here on earth.

I believe that in her heart of hearts, Jodi was first and foremost a mommy. Even though the cancer had ransacked her brain and messed up her speech and behaviors, she knew that her children needed access to her. As long as she was up in that tall hospital bed behind bars, there was no way her two little ones could get to her. So, despite what I'm sure cost her dearly in energy and caused her great pain, she continued to shimmy between the bars and plop on the floor so her children could get to her. She was undoubtedly as frustrated with Jim for putting her back in bed all the time as Jim was frustrated with her for continuing to "escape."

The next three days were a flurry of activity for Rick and Todd, preparing for the viewing and funeral. For me, it was about writing a speech for the funeral. I stayed in the hotel most of the time, coming out only to take the girls to the mall – a huge mistake for my heart, as every part of that mall reminded me of Jodi. But it was a distraction for Kaitlyn, and something I could do with the girls.

I managed to make it through the viewing dry-eyed. The funeral the following day was another matter. I was on the verge of tears at every image on the overhead screen of a vivacious and beautiful Jodi, and every glance at her darling children or Rick. I was a mess, and I had no idea how I was going to get through my eulogy. Just as I was about to go up to speak, Courtney leaned over to me and whispered, "Mom, please don't start crying when you get up there. You will make me cry." Okay then, I thought. No pressure there.

I asked Dawn, Jodi's best friend whom I had just met, to pray for me, and I sneaked out the back of the church to compose myself. As I stood in the back foyer, hearing the beautiful strains of the song

"Adonai," I looked out the window at the lovely blue Wisconsin sky and cried out to God. "You called me to this moment. You knew from the minute Jodi and I met in that hospital 3½ years ago that this moment would come to pass and I would be standing here about to speak at Jodi's final home-going. Every person in that sanctuary was touched in some way by Jodi and the beautiful way she chose to live her life. How can I summarize – in a mere 15 minutes – the friendship we shared, and all the other things we meant to each other as we battled side by side against cancer? God, please give me the strength and the words to share. I'm scrapping everything I've written down. Use me and fill my mouth with the words I need to speak for your glory and in Jodi's memory."

I went back into the church as I was introduced as if on cue. I shared. We laughed together at some of the stories I told. And many cried. I shared Jodi's faith and love for God. I shared about her love for her family. I shared her impact on my life, and how honored I felt to be called her friend. I told stories and I quoted scriptures and then I sat down. Amazingly, I never cried. I know it was God's words that came out of my mouth. Like Aaron of the Old Testament, I was simply God's mouthpiece. And that's how it was meant to be.

I will always carry Jodi close to my heart, and I am so blessed that God orchestrated our meeting and our friendship. I am a stronger person and a better Christian today because of the incredible impact of one little lady from Eau Claire, Wisconsin on my life. I will miss her until we meet again in heaven, but I will never regret the part of me that I invested in loving her.

We are still in touch with Rick and the kids.

# Chapter Twenty-One

There is no way to express in mere words the impact having cancer has had on my life, and the lives of my loved ones. But I can state, without hesitation, we have all learned many, many things. Todd and I were asked once if we wished we had never had to go though cancer. Without wavering, both of us answered, "No." We are so grateful for the lessons God has taught us through my having cancer.

Do we ever want to walk this journey again? "No!" But we wouldn't trade our lives for anyone else's; we wouldn't take it back and undo it if we had the chance.

I was speaking to a women's group after my second cancer, and I used the following illustration. I held up a spiral-bound notebook. "This is the 'story of Lori'," I began. "If you were to read this book, you would begin at my birth in chapter one and read on until you came to chapter 34, the age I was when I got cancer the first time. Chapters 34-37 would tell of the struggles and lessons I learned from having this awful disease. Then you would get to chapter 38, and the book would go on to chronicle my 'post-cancer' life. I often told

God that I would like to remove chapters 34-37 from my 'story of Lori' book. But He gripped my heart with some powerful truths. First, if I were to remove the chapters I didn't like, I would be insulting the Author of the whole book – God Himself! Second, if I were to rip out those chapters, everything from chapter 38 forward would make no sense. My life has been 'flavored' by cancer in such a momentous way that it permeates everything I do, and even who I am."

At the very beginning of my cancer journey, I said, "If I go through cancer and come out the other end the same person I was when I began, what was the point? I will have failed the test. But if I come through cancer and learn what God has for me to learn, and am a changed creation because of it, then God will be glorified and my struggles will not have been in vain."

# Index

i. Isaiah 55:8,9

ii. II Corinthians 12:9

iii. Hebrews 13:5

iv. Psalm 23:4

v. Hebrews 13:5

vi. Psalm 23:4

vii. Psalm 118:24

viii. Psalm 118:24

ix. song–sometimes He calms the storm but other times He calms the child.

x. Hebrews 13:5

xi. Psalm 23:4

xii. James 4:8